Where's Your Focus?

Writings of a Christian Optometrist

"Do not labor for the food which perishes, but for
the food which endures to everlasting life."
—John 6:27

JOSEPH W. SEGREE

WESTBOW®
PRESS
A DIVISION OF THOMAS NELSON
& ZONDERVAN

Scripture taken from the New King James Version. Copyright 1979, 1980, 1982 by Thomas Nelson, inc. Used by permission. All rights reserved.

WestBow Press books may be ordered through booksellers or by contacting:

WestBow Press
A Division of Thomas Nelson & Zondervan
1663 Liberty Drive
Bloomington, IN 47403
www.westbowpress.com
1 (866) 928-1240

ISBN: 978-1-4908-4732-0 (sc)
ISBN: 978-1-4908-4733-7 (e)

Library of Congress Control Number: 2014914052

Printed in the United States of America.

WestBow Press rev. date: 08/25/2014

To my wife, Alma, and our children, Angela Dayutis and Joe Segree, Jr.

Contents

* *

Section III: Letters

Section IV: Tracts

Preface

One of the great joys of being a Christian has been to write about it. For me, this has taken various forms: Bible study and journal notes, essays, sermons, booklets, gospel tracts, letters, and magazine articles. For a long time I have wanted to consolidate these writings in a way that would ensure their preservation and transmission to our descendants. *Where's Your Focus?* represents the fulfillment of this desire.

Two main themes can be seen in the pages that follow:

1. the importance of living an obedient Christian life through knowledge and application of the Scriptures; and
2. the biblical mandate to invest our lives in the spiritual well-being of others.

It seems that much of the busyness and activity of the Christian community may be without relevance and eternal significance. All ministry, indeed all activity in the church, must be evaluated in light of Christ's command to "bear fruit" for the kingdom of God. Biblically speaking, this is the definition of a life properly focused. It seems appropriate, therefore, that this book be entitled *Where's Your Focus?* This is also an allusion to the profession of optometry in which I have been occupied for most of my adult life.

Where's Your Focus? begins with excerpts from my Christian experience. The biblical groundwork, spiritual foundations, and lasting personal relationships instrumental in my development as a Christian have come from the times and events described in this section. The writings that follow are a product of these times and events as well.

I sincerely hope that you will find *Where's Your Focus?* meaningful, stimulating, and applicable to your own life. Toward this end, I am pleased to dedicate it to the praise and glory of our great God and Savior, Jesus Christ.

Acknowledgments

I would like to acknowledge my gratitude to the following people:

Alma, my wife—for her encouragement and support in the writing of this book and for her tireless assistance in editing the manuscript.

Howard Borland, Wayne Wright, Jim Webster, and Cecil Bean—the men who helped me find and keep my focus.

Clifford Brooks, Lon EuDaly, Mike Goen, Kelly Frantz, Dennis Cowley, and Dawn Kazmierzak—optometrists, brothers and sisters in Christ, and, for the past twenty-seven years, coworkers in the Fellowship of Christian Optometrists, International.

Jesus—the author and finisher of our faith.

SECTION I

Excerpts from
My Christian Experience

Parallel Paths

. . . .

"Therefore, my beloved brethren, be steadfast, immovable,
always abounding in the work of the Lord, knowing
that your labor is not in vain in the Lord."
—1 Corinthians 15:58

I am fortunate to have grown up in a God-fearing, Bible-believing family. My brother, sister, and I attended Sunday school regularly, though we did not always attend the worship service that followed. I received my first Bible at age five. It was a gift from my aunt, who was one of the church librarians. That Bible, which now sits on the bookshelf in my office, has, on its inside covers, a number of gold and silver stars, attendance stickers from my childhood Sunday school days. But I rarely opened it except to look at the pictures, sometimes reading a little on Sundays if the preacher or Sunday school teacher happened to arouse my interest in doing so.

When I was ten years old, my mother took me to talk to the pastor about becoming a member of the church, just as my brother and sister had done before me. The following Sunday morning, I went forward at the end of the worship service and was enthusiastically welcomed into the fellowship.

My understanding of the gospel at that time was nothing more than an intellectual belief that God had sent His Son Jesus Christ to die for our sins, and that a person must believe in Him to be saved. I believed what I had learned about Jesus in Sunday school: that He was the greatest man who ever lived, that He healed the sick and performed other miracles, and that He had been raised from the dead. Yet I did not know what it meant to have faith in Christ or to commit my life to Him. Unaware of the eternal consequences of sin or of the need to repent, I somehow passed the pastor's interrogation and was given the go-ahead to join the church. No doubt he presented me before the church that Sunday morning as one who had accepted Christ as my personal Savior, but I had not done so, though my intent was honest and sincere.

Twenty years later, Baptist Men's Day was being observed at Cahaba Heights Baptist Church in Birmingham, Alabama. On that annual event, the men of the church held a prayer breakfast, assembled a special choir, and conducted the morning worship service. Howard Borland, a layman from a nearby church, was the guest speaker. Following an inspirational music service, he spoke a challenging message to the men and women gathered that January day in 1975. A powerful movement of the Holy Spirit followed the invitation to accept Christ. Several people went forward to talk with the pastor. One man knelt and prayed with the speaker, while another was so emotionally overcome that he had to be carried out of the auditorium. An elderly gentleman found his way up into the choir loft, shouting, "God is still in the saving business!" There were tears, people embracing one another, and other expressions of joy and praise.

At that time, I was a twenty-nine-year-old, married optometry student with two small children. My wife, Alma, had begun serving as the minister of music at Cahaba Heights a few months earlier. I had become more and more involved in the church, attending Sunday school for the first time in many years. To an onlooker, there would have been no appearance or indication of my having been affected by the speaker's words or by the activity that followed. Yet somehow, in the midst of all that was taking place, I had quietly yielded my life to Christ and experienced a new kind of awareness—a realization that my sins had been forgiven and that the Holy Spirit had come into my life. I had been "born again" (John 3:3).

At Cahaba Heights, I quickly bonded with some men who were wholeheartedly devoted to impacting others for Jesus Christ: Wayne Wright, Harold Ward, and Kyle Floyd. I also found a like-minded man in Steve, the church youth director. Sharing a desire to tell others about Jesus, we sometimes went to malls and other places to pass out tracts and engage people with the gospel. We were bold, but not always wise. One day, we went through a large shopping mall, placing tracts on the benches and in public telephone booths. We stopped doing this after seeing a mall officer scoop up the tracts almost as fast as we could distribute them. Another one of our techniques was to go into bookstores and slip tracts inside certain types of books. I was particularly proud when I placed a tract inside *The Satanic Bible.* During my lunch hour, I walked through a university parking garage, inserting gospel tracts into open car windows. Two security guards soon appeared and told me to remove myself from the premises. That I did, glad to have been "persecuted for Christ's sake."

That was not the only time my efforts to share the gospel were thwarted. On weekends, I played in a band at a nearby country club. During my breaks, I would sometimes find inviting places for gospel tracts. After a few months, the band leader called and informed me that our group would no longer be playing there. I strongly suspected that I was the one who would no longer be playing there. Zeal for the gospel, if sometimes unbridled and a little reckless, brings its own reward—the satisfaction of having attempted to show people the way of salvation. I have never regretted the time and effort spent sharing the gospel of Jesus Christ.

My interest in gospel tracts had come from Howard Borland, who introduced me to this method of witnessing. Encouraged by his successful use of tracts as a ministry tool, I wrote the pamphlet "Share

Christ through Tract Evangelism," and later, a booklet called *Tracts, the Silent Evangelists.*

"This looks like a license to print money," remarked one of my optometry professors after examining my plan to open a practice in a small rural city. My family and I moved to Cadiz, Kentucky, eager to practice the profession for which I had been preparing over the past few years. Angela, our daughter, was almost six years old; Joe Jr. had just turned three. In a bold step of faith, we took out a bank loan and opened a private optometry office. The next few years were challenging from a business and financial standpoint (it was anything but a license to print money), but the practice grew, and we felt at home in Cadiz.

Within a month, we had joined Cadiz Baptist Church, where I was invited to teach a young adult Sunday school class. Not long afterward, we started a weeknight Bible study in our home, ministering both *inside* and *alongside* the local church—a practice we have continued ever since.

Not long after opening my optometry office, I wrote an evangelistic tract called "Our Eyes: A Christian Perspective." (Comparing natural and spiritual sight, this tract includes Bible verses that refer to eyes, light, and vision as metaphors for spiritual truth and understanding.) When I received a payment from one of my patients that was equal to the exact cost of having the tract printed, I took this as a sign of God's approval.

Ten years later, "Our Eyes" was adopted by the Fellowship of Christian Optometrists, an evangelical mission organization. Five thousand copies were printed initially; it was later translated into several other languages. This witnessing tool continues to be widely used today to present the gospel of Jesus Christ.

There is no record of how many copies of "Our Eyes" have been printed and distributed or of how many people, as a result of reading it, have come into a saving relationship with Jesus Christ. I am convinced, though, that God has indeed honored my desire to place it in His hands, claiming His promise: "So shall My word be that goes forth from My mouth; it shall not return to Me void, but it shall accomplish what I please, and it shall prosper in the thing for which I sent it" (Isaiah 55:11).

We had lived in Cadiz only a few months when I began to receive invitations to preach in some of the local churches when their pastors were away. After teaching Sunday school at our own church, I would hurry out to preach, Alma and the children often going with me. These were special times for our family.

A young man from one of those churches called and asked if he and I could meet. James was excited about the Christian life and wanted to talk with me about reaching others for Christ. I invited him to my office, eager to meet this man who had such a desire to witness. For the next year, we met regularly for Bible study and prayer, sometimes going out to witness. On one occasion, we attended a Bible rally in a neighboring city where he presented his salvation testimony, and I spoke on personal evangelism.

"I just got fired for witnessing," James told me. He had served in the military and was now working in a local factory. I knew that he witnessed with boldness, even in the workplace. "They didn't like me passing out tracts, so they let me go. They warned me that I should not be doing that, but I refused to compromise."

I commended him for his courage in standing by his convictions. "What do you plan to do now?" I asked.

"I think I'll go back to school." He enrolled in a nearby community college, but soon returned to military service.

The most significant event that resulted from my preaching in local churches was an invitation to serve as pastor of Canton Baptist Church, located a few miles from Cadiz. When I arrived there to preach one Sunday morning, R. C. Stallons, chairman of the pastor search committee, welcomed me with this question: "Joe, would you consider being our pastor?" (I had met R. C. and his wife, Jean, earlier when they came to my office for eye examinations.)

Alma and I were pleasantly surprised to learn that this church was considering me to be their pastor. After prayerful consideration, we felt that God was leading us there. We returned to Cahaba Heights Baptist Church in Birmingham for the ordination service. R. C. took part in the event, along with a number of pastors, deacons, and others we had known in Birmingham. Wayne Wright, my good friend and former Sunday school teacher, preached the ordination sermon.

At Canton, I was preaching two sermons a week, leading a midweek Bible study, and performing other pastoral duties. Meanwhile, I was practicing optometry full time. We quickly grew to love the men and women of Canton Baptist Church, who had graciously welcomed us into their family of faith. These were busy, but exciting, days! I later served as pastor of a small church in Mississippi. Today, I am the pastor of Raikes Hill Baptist Church near Campbellsville, Kentucky.

My spiritual growth and development during the years in Birmingham came mostly from reading and studying the Bible, reading Christian books, and listening to the teaching and preaching of a few men whom God brought into my life. I was hungry for things of the Lord. Soon after we moved to Kentucky, I was introduced to another resource for Christian growth and ministry.

My first awareness of The Navigators came by means of a booklet called *Born to Reproduce* by Dawson Trotman, who founded the Navigator organization in the early 1930s. The vision for spiritual multiplication presented in that booklet later became a significant part of my own ministry. In the fall of 1977, I discovered *Daws,* the biography of Dawson Trotman, by Betty Lee Skinner. I was so captivated by the life of this man of God that I read the entire four-hundred-page book in three days! The Navigators, a nondenominational, evangelical Christian organization that emerged from Trotman's pre-World War II ministry to sailors, had spread around the world. By then, Navigator work was being conducted on dozens of military bases and college campuses, among professional men and women, in the inner city, and in other venues.

Impressed as to the value of Scripture memory that I had read about in *Daws,* I enrolled in a correspondence course from Moody Bible Institute called "Memorize the Word." The course consisted of twelve lessons, each with six memory verses and a page of fill-in-the-blank study questions. The practice of memorizing Bible verses has been of enormous value to me through the years.

Another spiritual discipline that grew out of my encounter with The Navigators was the practice of a daily, disciplined time of Bible reading and prayer. I had been reading the Bible regularly for three years, but I had not yet begun to do so by means of a disciplined, systematic approach to the Scriptures. This "daily quiet time" that I began then continues to meet this need in my life today. (I have written about this subject in my booklet *How to Have an Effective Quiet Time.*)

I was leading a men's Bible study, meeting individually with a couple of guys, maintaining a meaningful quiet time, and memorizing Scripture, but one thing more was needed. I wanted to meet a real live "Navigator." I wrote to the organization in Colorado Springs, requesting the name of a staff member in my area. Jim Webster, the Navigator leader at Fort Knox, Kentucky, wrote back and referred me to Cecil Bean, director of the ministry at nearby Fort Campbell. These two men would deeply influence my walk with Christ for years to come, just as Howard Borland and Wayne Wright had done in Birmingham.

Cecil met with me regularly for the next four years, emphasizing the basics of one-on-one ministry and challenging me to reproduce my life, spiritually, in other men. I attempted to pass on the fundamentals of the Christian life that Cecil was modeling: a meaningful daily quiet time, how to study the Bible, Scripture memory, witnessing, giving, and the use of spiritual gifts. Through the years, I have continued to seek men who are willing to practice these spiritual disciplines and impart them to others.

My first Navigator conference took place in the fall of 1978 at Joe Wheeler State Park, near Florence, Alabama. There, I met Jim Webster, whose first words to me were these: "God is looking for a man of the Word, a man of faith, and a man of prayer." I wanted to be such a man! There would be other conferences, but that first one will always stand out as the time when I began to grasp the vision for man-to-man ministry that had guided the founder and early leaders of The Navigators. I was excited to be associated with men who were so focused upon evangelism and disciple-making.

In the years to come, I would work under the leadership of both Cecil and Jim in their respective ministries at Fort Campbell and Fort Knox. These men kept me supplied with audio tapes of speakers and teachers from other conferences and ministry events. They also involved me in their work of evangelism, teaching, and disciple-making. It seemed that I was partaking of a spiritual smorgasbord, and I loved it!

Jim Webster and I met regularly for more than twenty-five years until he went to be with the Lord in 2012. I cannot put a price on the example, encouragement, and wise counsel that I received from this godly man.

Early in my Christian life, there was a brief period when I wondered whether I should continue along the path toward an optometry career. The idea of a bi-vocational ministry was foreign to me at that time; I had not yet considered the notion of combining a life of Christian ministry with the practice of optometry. (My booklet *Life in the Marketplace* presents a biblical view of this concept.)

Many have the perception that lay people are the normal Christians, while the professionals—the clergy—are the "called ones," those who possess some greater spirituality or devotion to God. Martin Luther, the great sixteenth-century reformer, insisted that the public ministry was simply a matter of practical function or vocation, not a higher or more religious form of life with a special standing in God's eyes. We are all saved by the grace of God through faith and called to live in obedience to Jesus Christ. Yet some earn their living through Christian vocations, while most of us work in "secular" jobs.

One January morning in 1987, while walking from the parking lot to my office, I whispered a prayer that many have prayed: "Lord, I'm available. Show me how I can serve you more. I'll do whatever you want." Ten minutes later, thumbing through one of my professional journals, I came across the following advertisement: "Christian optometrist wanted for short-term mission work in Mombasa, Kenya." Convinced that God had directed me to that article, I wondered whether a trip to Kenya might be in the works for me. While such a trip was not to be, God did provide opportunities for me to participate in Christian eye care mission projects in Peru (three times), Ghana, and Costa Rica.

Glen Linsley, a Michigan optometrist, had placed that advertisement. Glen was on the board of directors of the Lighthouse for Christ Eye Centre, an eye hospital and clinic in Mombasa. I wasted no time calling him. Glen promised to send me an application to serve as a short-term missionary at the Lighthouse. He also referred me to Clifford Brooks, an optometrist at the Indiana University School of Optometry, who had recently founded an organization called the "Fellowship of Christian Optometrists, International" (FCO).

A few years earlier, I had conceived my own plan for a Christian optometry organization, with specific purposes and goals, a statement of faith, membership guidelines, and suggested activities. The "Christian Optometric Society" that I envisioned would soon merge into the already-established Fellowship of Christian Optometrists.

In our initial phone conversation, Cliff Brooks shared the history of FCO (only a year old at the time) and invited our family to his home to meet with some other members. A major decision at that meeting was to hold a conference for Christian optometrists and students. I volunteered to help plan the event, an overnight retreat held in November 1987 at McCormick's Creek State Park, near Bloomington, Indiana. Nineteen optometrists attended, along with family members and a few optometry students. (Today, FCO student chapters can be found in most of the schools and colleges of optometry in the United States.) The weekend was full: inspirational speakers, eye care mission presentations, continuing optometric education, student meetings, and a warm fellowship of like-minded Christian optometrists. The following year, it was expanded to a full weekend and has remained so ever since. Two years later, I accepted an invitation to join FCO's board of directors.

The Fellowship of Christian Optometrists is a nonprofit, evangelical organization of Christian optometrists, optometry students, and allied ophthalmic personnel committed to worldwide eye care missions and intra-professional Christian fellowship. Chief among its purposes is that of helping optometrists and other ophthalmic personnel become established in mission work that combines eye care and the advancement of the gospel of Jesus Christ.

Since we are not "professional clergy," we may be largely unrecognizable as ministers of the gospel, except by the testimony of Jesus Christ that we project in the workplace through our words and actions. A speaker at one of our conferences put it this way: "We are soldiers of Jesus Christ cleverly disguised as optometrists."

The Fellowship of Christian Optometrists has played a very significant role in my life. I could not have imagined what God had in store for me back in 1975 when I embarked upon the simultaneous pathways of "Christian ministry" and "a secular career." These pathways do indeed run parallel, and as followers of Jesus Christ, we can travel them both!

SECTION II
Journal Notes and Essays

Spiritual Vitality

· ·

"As newborn babes, desire the pure milk of the word
that you may grow thereby."
—1 Peter 2:2

Where there is life, there must be nourishment to sustain it and to produce growth and fruitfulness. Spiritual nourishment is just as vital to a healthy Christian life as food is to a healthy body. The plan for spiritual nourishment for a new Christian—indeed for every Christian—should include regular intake from the Bible. The most important thing we can do for new believers is to teach them how to feed themselves from the Word of God, beginning with a meaningful daily quiet time. Of course, we cannot expect from others what we are not practicing ourselves.

The Bible says, "And in this upper room, with his window open toward Jerusalem, he knelt down on his knees three times a day, and prayed, and gave thanks before his God, as was his custom since early days" (Daniel 6:10). In this verse, we see a pattern for prayer that the prophet Daniel had followed since childhood. It includes a set time, place, and plan for meeting with God. We would do well to follow this biblical model in our own devotional lives. There is simply no substitute for spending regular time in the Bible and prayer. The morning will be the best time of day for some, while the evening or lunch hour will be best for others.

How would you rate your devotional life as to its quality, regularity, and significance? Do you follow a plan for consistent reading through the Bible? Be careful not to substitute what others have written (as good and helpful as this may be) for reading the Bible itself. It will speak to the issues of your life. Begin your quiet time with a prayer, such as Psalm 119:18: "Open my eyes, that I might see wondrous things from Your law." Read the Bible, memorize verses, and meditate upon what you have read. Remember that "all Scripture is given by inspiration of God, and is profitable for doctrine, for reproof, for correction, for instruction in righteousness, that the man of God may be complete, thoroughly equipped for every good work" (2 Timothy 3:16).

The Universal Christian Experience

. . . .

"I was very diligent to write to you concerning
our common salvation."
—Jude 3

The apostle Paul and his party found some Christians at a place called Puteoli on the western coast of Italy. They were invited to stay with these brethren for seven days: "And so we went toward Rome. And from there, when the brethren heard about us, they came to meet us" (Acts 28:14–15). Who were these "brethren" that Luke, a companion of Paul, was describing? They were believers previously unknown to the apostle, yet they were men who had undoubtedly encountered Jesus Christ. When and by whom they had heard the gospel is unknown, yet that encounter with Christ had the same effect upon them as it had upon Paul, Luke, and the other believers in their party. As followers of Jesus Christ, they had obtained a "common salvation."

Since the days of the apostles, every genuine Christian has experienced the new birth, a spiritual regeneration brought about by the Holy Spirit. Meet a real Christian anywhere in the world, regardless of race, nationality, language, or culture, and you will find a person whose life has been profoundly changed by the power and presence of the living Christ. Every Christian possesses an inner light and peace that accompanies this "common salvation." We have had the same essential experience because we have been saved by the same God, through the same Savior, and by the same gospel.

Because the Holy Spirit of God dwells in us, we can relate to anyone who knows the power and presence of Jesus Christ in his life. This great truth may seem incomprehensible, yet we accept it by faith and know its reality beyond a doubt. Renowned Baptist theologian and educator E. Y. Mullins wrote:

> I have found, for me at least, irrefutable evidence of the objective existence of the Person so moving me. When to this personal experience I add that of tens of thousands of living Christians, and an unbroken line of them back to Christ, and when I find in the New Testament a manifold record of like experiences, together with a clear account of the origin and cause of them all, my certainty becomes absolute.[1]

The Christian experience is universal, unique, and irrefutable.

Redemptive Ministry

. . . .

"He has sent redemption to His people."
—Psalm 111:9

A Christian should regard every human relationship as "redemptive." He or she must want the other person to know Jesus Christ as Savior and Lord.

Jesus' life was focused upon the kingdom of God and the needs of people. He showed us how to make redemptive ministry a way of life. The manner in which we do this depends upon a number of factors: our spiritual gifts, the desires of our heart, our willingness to confront people with the gospel, and the opportunities that come along.

We are engaged in redemptive ministry whenever we talk to people about Jesus Christ—when we exhort them to read the Bible, invite them to church, or pray for them. We are behaving in a redemptive manner when we help the impoverished; encourage the fainthearted; visit the sick, lonely, and imprisoned; and when we extend other acts of kindness in the name of Jesus.

But redemptive ministry is more than just performing certain acts; there is a redemptive aspect to simply living an obedient Christian life that others can see. The expression "lifestyle evangelism" conveys the meaning of redemptive ministry. Our goal is to win people to Jesus Christ, but we seldom begin by sharing the gospel. Rather, we befriend people and develop relationships with them. It is out of these relationships that we gain opportunities to share.

Paul wrote these words to the Christians at Thessalonica: "But we were gentle among you, just as a nursing mother cherishes her own children. So, affectionately longing for you, we were well pleased to impart to you not only the gospel of God, but also our own lives, because you had become dear to us" (1 Thessalonians 2:7–8).

In one way or another, we should always be about the business of pointing people toward Jesus.

The Ministry of Encouragement

"We sent Timothy to encourage you concerning your faith."
—1 Thessalonians 3:2

When Joseph arrived in Antioch "and saw the evidence of the grace of God, he was glad and encouraged them all to remain true to the Lord with all their hearts" (Acts 11:23). The apostles had given him the name Barnabas, which means "Son of Encouragement" (Acts 4:36).

It has been said that, in one way or another, "encouraging others" is what ministry is all about. It is a part of the disciple-making process and encompasses many aspects of it. The training of disciples and disciple-makers requires much more than just words, but it can begin with one person simply encouraging another. It should also be a natural expression of our love and concern for fellow believers.

The Bible commands us to encourage one another: "And let us consider one another in order to stir up love and good works, not forsaking the assembling of ourselves together, as is the manner of some, but exhorting (*encouraging*) one another, and so much the more as you see the Day approaching" (Hebrews 10:24–25 emphasis mine).

One goal of encouraging people is to help them become all that they feel God wants them to become.

Encouragement can take many forms: "Hang in there! You can do it!" "Be sure to read the Bible every day." "I enjoy spending time with you." "You're such an asset to our Sunday school class." There is no end to the encouraging things that we can say to others. We must never underestimate the impact that a few well-chosen or well-timed words can have on someone. "A word fitly spoken is like apples of gold in settings of silver" (Proverbs 25:11).

Even the memory of a person who lived an exemplary Christian life can be a great encouragement. This is the case with Howard Borland, the man whom I credit with having led me to Christ and Jim Webster, my spiritual mentor for nearly twenty-five years.

Who looks to you for encouragement?

Another View of Fellowship

"The hearts of the saints have been refreshed by you, brother."
—Philemon 7

Fellowship means union among "fellows," or brethren. We cannot live in spiritual isolation—we need other believers. In this brief letter to Philemon, Paul mentions eleven different Christian brothers who were, in some way, a part of his ministry. He refers to Philemon, Mark, Aristarchus, Demas, and Luke as "fellow laborers" (Philemon 1, 24).

The Christian life, when lived in obedience to God, is a life of spiritual labor. We labor to grow in our relationship with Jesus Christ through the disciplines of prayer and Bible study. We labor in our daily effort to provide for our families. We labor as we minister to people in the name of Jesus. But we cannot do this alone—we are fellow laborers with our brothers and sisters in Christ.

Paul names Archippus as a "fellow soldier" (Philemon 2), serving together in spiritual warfare against the god of this world: the devil. We, too, are soldiers in God's army, called daily to fight against spiritual forces—those whose aim is to destroy the kingdom of God and neutralize our effectiveness in the world. The apostle Paul calls Epaphras his "fellow prisoner" (Philemon 23), as enslaved together to a single master—the Lord Jesus Christ.

Fellowship is vital to a healthy Christian experience. One can be saved, perhaps, and continue to exist without fellowship, but he or she cannot mature spiritually or be effective in ministry. The "communion of the Holy Spirit" (2 Corinthians 13:14) operates through believers living and serving together in the cause of Christ as fellow laborers, fellow soldiers, and fellow prisoners. Thus Paul writes to the Philippians: "I thank my God upon every remembrance of you… for your fellowship in the gospel from the first day until now" (Philippians 1:3, 5).

Can it be said of you that "the hearts of the saints have been refreshed by you"?

Eternal Accountability

"So then, each of us will give an account of himself to God."
—Romans 14:12

The message of the gospel is that "God so loved the world that He gave His only begotten Son, that whoever believes in Him should not perish but have everlasting life" (John 3:16).

This is the basis of our eternal hope. We who have trusted Christ are saved by God's grace and will be transformed into the likeness of Christ when He returns. We will spend eternity in heaven, where Christ is at the right hand of God, interceding for us (Hebrews 7:25).

Yet in the face of this glorious truth, there is a further consideration to which we must pay careful attention. It is quite clear from the Scriptures that even for the Christian, there is to be a day of recompense. These words of the apostle Paul speak directly to both the present and future life of a Christian: "For we must all appear before the judgment seat of Christ, that each one may receive what is due him for the things done while in the body, whether good or bad" (2 Corinthians 5:10). All believers, whether living or dead at Christ's coming, must face him in judgment. Grace does not eliminate accountability. There are eternal consequences for temporal behavior. Every child of God must therefore examine the conduct of his or her life in light of this profound biblical truth.

Sometimes a biblical truth begins to take on a new and greater significance as we earnestly consider its implications for our lives.

23

This was the case for me regarding the biblical teaching about eternal accountability. Even though we who have trusted Christ as our Savior will spend eternity in heaven, the state or quality of that existence will be determined in part by the degree to which we obey and serve God in this life. As followers of Jesus Christ, we must heed this teaching carefully in light of its profound eternal implications. It is not enough just to repent and receive Him as Savior. God calls us to a life of obedience!

One day, we will answer for how we have responded to this call. We must invest wisely now, pressing "toward the goal for the prize of the upward call of God in Christ Jesus" (Philippians 3:14).

A Strange Inversion

"But he who is greatest among you shall be your
servant. And whoever exalts himself will be humbled,
and he who humbles himself will be exalted."
—Matthew 23:11–12

A strange inversion can be found in the program of God. According to Jesus, the first will be last, and the last will be first. The one who loves his life will lose it, and the one who hates his life will keep it. In order to live, one must first die. He who humbles himself will be exalted. He who serves others will be exalted. A close reading of the Gospels reveals many examples of this inversion (reversal) of the normal order of things.

Jesus said, "If anyone desires to come after Me, let him deny himself, and take up his cross, and follow Me. For whoever desires to save his life will lose it, but whoever loses his life for My sake will find it" (Matthew 16:24–25). Mark writes: "And He sat down, called the twelve, and said to them, 'If anyone desires to be first, he shall be last of all and servant of all.' Then He took a little child and set him in the midst of them. And when He had taken him in His arms, He said to them, 'Whoever receives one of these little children in My name receives Me; and whoever receives Me, receives not Me but Him who sent Me'" (Mark 9:35–37).

Jesus spoke these words not long before His death: "Most assuredly, I say to you, unless a grain of wheat falls into the ground and dies, it remains alone; but if it dies, it produces much grain. He who loves his

25

life will lose it, and he who hates his life in this world will keep it for eternal life. If anyone serves Me, let him follow Me; and where I am, there My servant will be also. If anyone serves Me, him My Father will honor" (John 12:24–26).

In response to the disciples' dispute over greatness, Jesus said, "The kings of the Gentiles exercise lordship over them, and those who exercise authority over them are called 'benefactors.' But not so among you; on the contrary, he who is greatest among you let him be as the younger, and he who governs as he who serves. For who is greater, he who sits at the table, or he who serves? Is it not he who sits at the table? Yet I am among you as the One who serves" (Luke 22:25–27).

Finally, it is written in the Gospel of John: "So when He had washed their feet, taken His garments, and sat down again, He said to them, 'Do you know what I have done to you? You call Me Teacher and Lord, and you say well, for so I am. If I then, your Lord and Teacher, have washed your feet, you also ought to wash one another's feet. For I have given you an example, that you should do as I have done to you. Most assuredly, I say to you, a servant is not greater than his master; nor is he who is sent greater than he who sent him'" (John 13:13–16).

Indeed, Jesus is the supreme example of this strange inversion, but it can also be found in the Christian who follows His example.

Investing in Eternity

"So teach us to number our days, that we
may gain a heart of wisdom."
—Psalm 90:12

It has been said that in order to know how rich we are, we can add up everything in our lives that money cannot buy and death cannot take away. These, our true riches, will last forever, while everything else is temporary and will pass away. Jesus said, "Do not lay up for yourselves treasures on earth, where moth and rust destroy and where thieves break in and steal; but lay up for yourselves treasures in heaven, where neither moth nor rust destroys and where thieves do not break in and steal. For where your treasure is, there your heart will be also" (Matthew 6:19–21). Our devotion to Christ and His kingdom can be measured by the degree to which we invest what God has given us: money, material possessions, time, natural talents, opportunities, and relationships.

Jesus spoke not only about heavenly "treasure," but also about heavenly "labor." He fed more than five-thousand people on a Galilean mountainside. The masses continued to follow Him, for they saw in Him a way to have their physical needs met. It was on that occasion that Jesus exhorted His disciples with these words: "Do not labor for the food which perishes, but for the food which endures to everlasting life, which the Son of Man will give you, because the Father has set his seal of approval on Him" (John 6:27).

A man was studying to become a civil engineer in order to build highways and bridges. In time, he discovered 2 Peter 3:10, where God promises that one day, He will destroy everything the man hoped to build. Not wanting to invest his life in something God would surely destroy, he gave up engineering and entered the ministry.

The Bible speaks of two things that will endure forever: the Word of God and the souls of people. A life spent in the service of Jesus Christ on behalf of people, bringing the Word of God to them, will ensure reward in heaven. Our task as Christians is to help populate heaven by sharing the gospel. We lay up treasure in heaven anytime we lead people to Jesus Christ and whenever we minister to them in His name. The Bible says, "And whoever gives one of these little ones only a cup of cold water in the name of a disciple, assuredly, I say to you, he shall by no means lose his reward" (Matthew 10:42). We can do nothing greater to ensure that heavenly treasure will be credited to our account.

Only in heaven will we know the extent to which we have impacted others for Christ. As we lay up treasure in heaven, may we be able to say, like the apostle Paul, "For what is our hope, or joy, or crown of rejoicing? Is it not even you in the presence of our Lord Jesus Christ at His coming? For you are our glory and joy" (1 Thessalonians 2:19–20).

Living by Faith

· ·

"For we walk by faith, not by sight."
—2 Corinthians 5:7

Faith relates to the unseen and to the future. According to the Bible, "Now faith is the substance of things hoped for, the evidence of things not seen" (Hebrews 11:1). Our faith must cause us to act on the promises and commands of Scripture, but it is our trust in God Himself that counts. Even when we do not understand His promises and commands, we must have faith in His character. The essential thing is the "faithfulness of God." Jesus' words, "Have faith in God" (Mark 11:22), have also been translated as saying, "Hold onto the faithfulness of God."

Without faith, it is impossible to please God. He rewards those who diligently (by faith) seek Him (Hebrews 11:6). Since God is invisible, we can know Him only by faith. As we exercise this trust, we help determine the way things go in our lives. Jesus told the blind men, as He restored their sight, "According to your faith let it be to you" (Matthew 9:29). He said to the woman with a flow of blood, "Your faith has made you well" (Matthew 9:22).

Faith and sight are mutually exclusive. Paul expressed a similar idea: "Hope that is seen is not hope; for why does one hope for what he sees? For if we hope for what we do not see, we eagerly wait for it with perseverance" (Romans 8:24–25). Faith can only be nourished by hope. Paul was referring to the Lord Jesus Christ when he wrote,

"Through whom we have access by faith into this grace in which we stand, and rejoice in hope of the glory of God" (Romans 5:1–2). In this way, biblical faith and biblical hope go together. In the New Testament, hope refers to favorable and confident expectation. Like faith, it has to do with the unseen and the future.

We do not need signs from God to affirm His presence or power—our faith establishes this beyond any doubt. Living by faith does not mean that we can throw away reason and common sense or that we can neglect caution. But when reason can take us no further, we proceed by faith. This involves risks that we would not otherwise take. Assuming that the revelation of God in Scripture can be trusted—a presupposition central to the Christian faith—a biblical faith can be exercised with confidence and assurance.

Humility

. . . .

"God resists the proud, but gives grace to the humble."
—1 Peter 5:5

[This article is taken from my booklet *The Meaning of Greatness*.]

Jesus referred to little children when teaching important truths about the kingdom of heaven: "Let the little children come to Me, and do not forbid them; for of such is the kingdom of heaven" (Matthew 19:14). According to Matthew, "Jesus called a little child to Him, set him in the midst of them, and said, 'Assuredly, I say to you, unless you are converted and become as little children, you will by no means enter the kingdom of heaven. Therefore whoever humbles himself as this little child is the greatest in the kingdom of heaven'" (Matthew 18:2–4).

Little children are innocent, submissive, dependent, and trusting. Just as they are a source of joy to their parents and grandparents, we, too, should be a joy to our heavenly Father. Our lives should likewise be marked by innocence, submission, dependence, and trust. These characteristics of a little child reveal something about humility.

What is humility? From a biblical perspective, it is not as some believe—a belittling of oneself; rather, it is an exalting or praising of others, especially God and Jesus Christ. Biblical humility is also recognizing that by ourselves, we are inadequate, without dignity, and worthless. Since God is both our Creator and Redeemer, our existence and righteousness come from Him. Yet because we are created in God's

31

image, as believers in Christ, we possess infinite worth and dignity. True humility does not produce pride, but gratitude. The humble mind is at the root of all other graces and virtues. Self-exaltation spoils everything. There can be no real love without humility. "Love," said Paul, "suffers long and is kind; love does not envy; love does not parade itself, is not puffed up; does not behave rudely, does not seek its own…" (1 Corinthians13:4–5).

Jesus said, "Blessed are the poor in spirit, for theirs is the kingdom of heaven" (Matthew 5:3). Dwight Hill says,

> By "poor in spirit" Christ meant the spiritually destitute, those who acknowledge their utter helplessness, spiritual poverty, and lack of superiority before others—people who are painfully aware of their deadness before God. The "poor in spirit" recognize that they are no better, no richer, no more superior to the next person, regardless of what they have achieved in this world in terms of fame, fortune, or power.[2]

In the following graphic description of what it means to be humble, Brennan Manning refers to the "poor in spirit" as "ragamuffin" believers:

> The unsung assembly of saved sinners who are little in their own sight, conscious of their brokenness and powerlessness before God, and who cast themselves on his mercy. Startled by the extravagant love of God, they do not require success, fame, wealth, or power to validate their worth. Their spirit transcends all distinctions between the powerful and powerless, educated and illiterate, billionaires and bag ladies, high-tech geeks and low-tech nerds, males and females, the circus and the sanctuary.[3]

An elderly minister was asked to explain the secret of a lifetime of successful Christian ministry. His response was, "I have always sought obscurity and given God the glory!" He was echoing the psalmist, who wrote, "Not unto us, O LORD, not unto us, but to Your name give glory, because of Your mercy, because of Your truth" (Psalm 115:1). This is humility.

But humility does not mean letting others walk over you. We can be sure that Jesus would not have been accused of being humble when He made a whip and cleansed the temple of those who were buying and selling sacrificial animals (John 2:14–17). Nor would John the Baptist have been regarded as particularly humble when he called the Pharisees and Sadducees "a brood of vipers" and provoked them with his message of repentance. Humility does not prevent us from expressing righteous anger or taking a stand for the truth and commands of God.

The Normal Christian Life

"And the disciples were first called Christians in Antioch."
—Acts 11:26

The word "normal" can be simply defined as "how things should be." The normal way to boil an egg is to heat it in water to 212 degrees Fahrenheit. There may be some other way, but this is the normal way. A teacher will tell you that most of the students in a classroom would be considered normal.

What constitutes a normal Christian life? Keep in mind that one must first *be* a Christian before he or she can be a "normal" Christian. Paul said, "Examine yourselves as to whether you are in the faith" (2 Corinthians 13:5). A normal Christian is, first of all, a believer, one who has entered into a personal relationship with Jesus Christ.

We tend to place Christians into two categories: (1) ordinary men and women, the rank-and-file members of the church; and (2) professional ministers, or clergy. For many, there is the perception that the lay people are the normal Christians, while the professionals are something more. The professionals are often regarded as the "called ones," men and women who possess some greater devotion to God and are, thereby, beyond normal. However, the Bible declares all believers to be priests (1 Peter 2:9 and Revelation 1:6). Contrary to tradition and centuries of church teaching, the Bible makes no distinction between the nonvocational and the vocational (professional) ministry.

The principle difference between professional ministers and the rest of us is in how we earn our living. It is simply a matter of funding. But we are all saved by the grace of God through faith and are called to live in obedience to Jesus Christ. This is the normal Christian life.

Fruit That Remains

. . . .

"You did not choose Me, but I chose you and appointed you that
you should go and bear fruit, and that your fruit should remain."
—John 15:16

These words that Jesus spoke to His disciples are especially relevant to
those of us who are evangelical, mission-minded Christians. Whether
at home or on the foreign mission field, nothing we do in the area of
Christian missions will mean much if there are no lasting results. It
is imperative that we conserve the fruits of evangelism, and from that
harvest, build up foundations for spiritual generations.

It is a healthy practice to slow down sometimes and consider all of
our efforts in the area of Christian ministry. Are we bearing fruit, and if
so, is it fruit that remains? What we regard as "ministry" may, in some
cases, be nothing more than Christian activity. It may be good in itself,
yet it may bear no lasting fruit.

Much of what we do in the name of Jesus Christ may show no signs
of lasting results, yet we minister in obedience to the Word of God with
the assurance that our "labor is not in vain in the Lord" (1 Corinthians
15:58). We should see the fruit of our labor in the permanently changed
lives of the people to whom we have ministered and by their influence
for Christ in the lives of others.

When Jesus told His disciples to go and "make disciples of all
nations," He set into motion His plan for world evangelism. The first
disciples and the early church were obedient to that command, and the

body of Christ experienced phenomenal growth. Individual disciples reproduced their lives in others, while churches reproduced through the planting of new churches.

A disciple is one who learns by following another. A true disciple of Jesus Christ must be established in the Word, prayer, witnessing, and fellowship. Are you a disciple of Jesus Christ? Are you walking in obedience to His Word? Are you established in the Word, prayer, witnessing, and fellowship? If not, then strive for this goal, and help someone else do the same. This may be the greatest contribution that you can make toward the fulfillment of the Great Commission.

Jesus has chosen us and wants to send us forth to bear lasting fruit for His kingdom. Ask Him to bring someone along who has a desire to grow as a Christian, one who has a desire to help others. Trust Him and see what He will do through your life.

Losing Sight of Lordship

"Whoever desires to come after Me, let him deny himself,
and take up his cross, and follow Me."
—Mark 8:34

[This article is taken from my booklet *The Problem of Tares*.]

For many, being a Christian is like the teenage boy who wants all that he can get from his father, but he refuses to accept and yield to parental authority. He wants to drive the family car on Friday and Saturday nights, but he chooses not to obey the midnight curfew imposed by his father. He enjoys the comfort of a nice home, but he rebels when told to take out the trash and clean his room. He expects a weekly allowance, but he ignores his father's advice on how to use it.

Many people want the security of salvation, but they rebel against God's rule in their lives. They do not understand what it means to obey the gospel. Lordship is not in their vocabulary. In *True Discipleship*, William MacDonald says:

> True Christianity is an all-out commitment to the Lord Jesus Christ. The Savior is not looking for men and women who will give their spare evenings to Him—or their weekends or retirement years. Rather he seeks those who will give Him first place in their lives."[4]

We must not wait until retirement to give Him first place in our lives, nor should we serve Christ only until we reach retirement age. We must never adopt the attitude that we have "done our part" and can now "hand it over to the next generation."

John Stott puts it this way:

> The astonishing idea is current in some circles today that we can enjoy the benefits of Christ's salvation without accepting the challenge of His sovereign lordship. Such an unbalanced notion is not to be found in the New Testament. "Jesus is Lord" is the earliest known formulation of the creed of Christians. In days when imperial Rome was pressing its citizens to say "Caesar is Lord," these words had a dangerous flavor. But Christians did not flinch. They could not give Caesar their first allegiance, because they had already given it to Emperor Jesus.[5]

The Christian life is one of obedience! Anything less than absolute surrender to the lordship of Christ and unswerving obedience to His Word falls short of God's plan for those who would be Christ's disciple. It is essential, therefore, that every believer submit to the terms of discipleship laid out by the Lord Jesus Christ. Where the Church has lost sight of lordship and failed to emphasize obedience in conjunction with salvation, it has paid dearly, for what remains are weak congregations made up largely of spiritually unproductive members.

Where lordship is separated and excluded from the message of salvation, those who would follow Christ are destined for failure. These people become comfortable with a form of Christianity in which they are never challenged to an all-out surrender of their lives to Christ. Theirs is an easy, inauthentic Christianity—an imitation of the real thing. Where obedience to the Word is not stressed, most Christians stand little chance of experiencing true lordship, and as a result, they fail to grow and never produce spiritual fruit.

A Holy God

It was essential from the outset that the people of God glorify Him and regard Him as holy. When Aaron's two eldest sons, Nadab and Abihu, offered unauthorized fire on the altar, God destroyed them without warning (Leviticus 10:1–3). He then commanded that neither Moses, Aaron, nor anyone else in Israel should mourn the loss of those wicked men. The Bible does not tell us what this "unauthorized fire" consisted of, but it is clear that it violated God's plan for worship. God's action was a warning to any Israelite who would consider straying from His exact prescription for worship.

Some find it tedious to read certain parts of the Old Testament. Consider, for example, God's plan for constructing the tabernacle; the details regarding the priestly garments and functions; instructions about sacrifices and offerings; and laws pertaining to foods. We may wonder why God ordered such things and whether they have any practical relevance for us today. Certainly, we can be thankful that we are not burdened with such cumbersome requirements for worship, for maintaining our relationship with God, and for fellowship with other Christians. In a way which we may not fully understand, these things that God prescribed are actually a reflection of His holiness. In our worship today, we must always recognize God's holiness and give Him the praise, honor, and glory due Him.

God sometimes acted decisively and without warning in dealing with those who disobeyed or rebelled against Him, as in the case of Nadab and Abihu. (Could this be the reason for some of the unexpected and unexplained adversity in people's lives today?) This may seem harsh—that God would destroy Aaron's sons without warning and then forbid others from mourning their deaths. However, when we consider that God is the Creator and Sustainer of the universe, this action should suggest something to us about His indescribable holiness, and in comparison, our utter sinfulness. We must pursue holiness in our own lives: "As He who called you is holy, you also be holy in all your conduct" (1 Peter 1:15).

Fortunately, we are no longer bound by the Old Testament system of sacrifices. Jesus Christ completed that ministry once and for all: "For by one offering He has perfected forever those who are being sanctified" (Hebrews 10:14). Yet God is the same as in the days of Moses, and so now, as then, we are to glorify Him and treat Him as holy. To do otherwise may be to risk decisive and unexpected consequences!

Only One Truth

"The entirety of Your word is truth."
—Psalm 119:160a

The adherents of any religion will undoubtedly believe their religion to be true, just as Christians do. But believing in a religion does not make it so. Christianity is true not because we embrace it; we embrace it because it is true! In other words, truth is truth, whether we believe it or not. A man drives his tractor onto an ice-covered pond, believing that the ice is strong enough to hold it. Another refuses to do so because he does not believe that it will support the tractor. The truth about the ice (whether it is two feet or only two inches thick) does not depend upon, nor is it affected by, the beliefs of the two men. There is only one truth about the thickness and strength of the ice.

Jesus said, "I am the way, the truth, and the life. No one comes to the Father except through Me" (John 14:6). Christianity reflects the truth about God, salvation, and eternity. Again, this is so whether we believe it or not.

There are some profound differences between Christianity and all other religions and systems of religious belief:

1. Christianity alone is founded upon God's revelation to the human race. All other religions are based upon some form of human effort.

2. Christianity is founded upon a person—Jesus Christ! As it says in the Bible, "Who do you say that I am?... You are the Christ, the Son of the living God" (Matthew 16:15–16).

3. Christianity alone can claim an empty tomb for its founder.

There may be Buddhists who have more faith in Buddha than some Christians have in Christ. The same can be said about the followers of Mohammed, Confucius, and the founders of other religions. But the Christian is saved, not because of the amount of his faith, but because of the One in whom he has placed his faith! A deranged man may think he can safely jump out of an airplane without a parachute, and he may sincerely believe that he will be unharmed. On the other hand, a man with just the slightest faith in the parachute will descend safely to the ground if he will commit himself to it. The Bible says that a person who has as much faith in Christ as that represented by tiny mustard seed can be saved because his faith is placed in the right object. To the contrary, the Muslim, Hindu, and Buddhist will miss heaven altogether because their faith is not in the only One who can save them.

Finally, the notion that the many religions of the world are just different ways to God is absolutely false! Man cannot invent ways to God. We come to Him only by faith in the Lord Jesus Christ.

What about the Heathen?

"For the invisible things of Him from the creation of the world are clearly seen, being understood by the things that are made, even His eternal power and Godhead, so that they are without excuse."
—Romans 1:20

One of the first questions I had to answer as I began to consider the claims of Christianity was this: "What about the heathen—the people around the world who have never heard about Jesus Christ? Why should they receive eternal punishment for not accepting a Savior and a God about whom they have never heard?" This is one of the questions most often used by skeptics to reject the truth of the Christian faith. Many cannot conceive of a loving God who would condemn people that never had an opportunity to trust Christ.

We cannot use this issue as an indictment against God or to judge Him on the basis of our limited knowledge. We must instead answer the question in light of what we do know about God. The Bible teaches that God is "just." Whatever happens to the heathen or to anyone else is the result of His righteous judgment. It is reassuring to know that the eternal destiny of those who die without having heard the message of salvation is in the hands of the One who is fair and just.

People are not condemned only after hearing the gospel and rejecting it, but on the basis of their sins: "He who believes in Him is not condemned; but he who does not believe is condemned already, because he has not believed in the name of the only begotten Son of God" (John

3:18). The heathen are no more entitled to escape God's condemnation than those who have heard the gospel and rejected it. The Bible says that all have sinned and stand condemned without Jesus Christ.

God has revealed Himself to all people through both nature and conscience, yet most have failed to honor Him as God and are, therefore, "without excuse" with respect to eternal judgment. While most men fail to seek God, the Bible seems to indicate that those who genuinely do so will find Him. Perhaps this is why we read stories of missionaries who encounter primitive tribes of people worshiping the true and living God, even though they have never been exposed to missionaries or received the written Word.

Finally, never assume that the heathen can be found only in unevangelized foreign lands. They may be in your neighborhood, your workplace, your school, or even in your family. In one sense, the heathen are those who have never heard the gospel; in another sense, they are all people who are without Christ and in the darkness of sin. Remember: we ourselves were at one time without Christ, "strangers from the covenants of promise, having no hope and without God in the world" (Ephesians 2:12).

Abandoning the Newborn

* *

"For everyone who partakes only of milk is unskilled
in the word of righteousness, for he is a babe."
—Hebrews 5:13

[This article is taken from my booklet *The Problem of Tares*.]

The needs of a new Christian are much like those of a newborn baby: love, food, and protection. After the assurance of salvation, he needs love and acceptance by the body of Christ. He must be fed spiritually and taught how to feed himself from the Word of God. He must be protected from whatever would harm him, but especially from Satan's efforts to destroy his faith and hinder his Christian growth.

Pastors and evangelists agree that those who make decisions to follow Christ must be encouraged and helped to grow in their relationship with Him. They must not be allowed to come to the threshold of the kingdom of God and then be lost for lack of proper nurturing. No ministry should be more important to the life of a church than that of following up on decisions for Christ. Whether this is done through an organized program or by the personal ministry of a few dedicated men and women, it must be given top priority.

Jesus said, "What man of you, having a hundred sheep, if he loses one of them, does not leave the ninety-nine in the wilderness, and go after the one which is lost until he finds it?" (Luke 15:4). Many churches today seem content to let not just the one, but the ninety-nine, wander away in the event that much effort is required to keep and protect them. As long as decisions for Christ are seen as statistics rather than as evidence of souls seeking salvation, there will be very little incentive for follow-up. God forbid that the leaders of any church that confesses Jesus Christ as Lord would lack either the ability or the willingness to provide the nurturing necessary to establish new converts in the faith!

A busy pastor may know that he must get around to implementing "that all-important follow-up program for new Christians," but too often, it gets edged out by other programs and activities. There may be nobody who is willing to work in this area of ministry. As a result, new believers often receive woefully inadequate nurturing, or else they are simply abandoned altogether.

One element of Satan's strategy for hindering the growth of the church is to see that those who want to follow Christ are never given the opportunity to "come alive" spiritually. If he can keep them out of the Bible, he can stop the growth process before it begins. It is the Word of God that gives life, and Satan knows it!

Busy Here and There

* *

"A man came over and brought a man to me, and said, 'Guard
this man; if by any means he is missing, your life shall be
for his life, or else you shall pay a talent of silver.' While
your servant was busy here and there, he was gone."
—1 Kings 20:39–40

[This article is taken from my booklet *The Problem of Tares*.]

Eternity may reveal the number of people who are lost forever because
the church was "busy here and there." They may not be gone physically;
they attend church regularly, but they are gone spiritually because they
do not know Christ. Dawson Trotman, founder of The Navigators,
refers to the busyness of the church as "the curse of today, busy doing
Christian things: spiritual activity with little productivity."[6] Much of
the feverish and frustrating activity of the contemporary church may be
without relevance and fulfillment. All ministry, indeed all activity, in
the church must be evaluated in light of the biblical mandate to "bear
fruit" for the kingdom of God (John 15:16). Stated another way, it must
be redemptive.

Some activities are inherently redemptive: worship services,
Bible studies, prayer meetings, mission work, ministry training, and
evangelism. Other activities may be redemptive only when they are
made to be so: health and fitness, sports, arts and crafts, drama, and
church outings.

This is not to say that most church programs and activities do not, in some way, contribute to the edifying of the body or the evangelizing of the unsaved—only that they are but lifeless activities if they do not. Unfortunately, church priorities are often shifted in favor of things which are the least productive from an eternal perspective. The result is that more and more Christians confuse Christian activity with spiritual productivity, and fewer unsaved members ever come to know Christ personally.

In order to carry on the broad range of activities often expected of large churches today, many have activity centers staffed by full-time ministers. While these may play a significant role in the accomplishment of the churches' primary tasks, they may also lose their redemptive emphasis if not monitored properly. I know of a large church that conducted a daytime ministry for dozens of inner city youth. While the church facility provided many worthwhile activities, there were times when secular, even unwholesome music, could be heard there. Television programs with ungodly themes and improper language were sometimes played, while volunteer workers would interact with the youth in a manner more like that of a secular club than a Christian ministry.

Worship services must not be dominated by entertainment without spiritual relevance, nor should Sunday school classes devote more time to refreshments, socializing, announcements, and the planning of activities than to Bible study.

One thing that sets the church apart from service clubs and community groups is that it is not just an organization, but a living organism whose mission is redemptive. I once belonged to a civic club that met once a week for lunch, business, and a program. I looked forward to the meetings, enjoyed the programs, and felt good about the worthwhile community service that the club performed. But it did not compare to the church, with its weekly worship services, the preaching and teaching of the Bible, the fellowship of believers, and various ministry opportunities. We must be careful not to let the church become a Sunday morning club.

The church must not be satisfied with doing things that are good in place of things that are essential. While we should not neglect legitimate things of lesser importance, we must never lose sight of the essentials—salvation of the lost, training of disciples, and building up of the body of Christ in other ways. We must be careful about being "busy here and there," for in so doing, we may deprive some of a genuine salvation experience and a lifetime of meaningful Christian service.

The Process of
Disciple-Making

* *

"And the number of the disciples multiplied greatly in Jerusalem."
—Acts 6:7

Jesus commanded the apostles to "go make disciples." In light of the many references in the Gospels and Acts to those who were called "disciples," we might expect disciple-making to be a major theme in the writings of Paul, Peter, John, and the others. Yet the words "disciple," "disciple-making," and "discipleship" are curiously absent from the New Testament epistles.

What is a disciple? A disciple is, foremost, a learner—one who follows the teachings of another. A disciple of Jesus Christ is one who is ever learning from Him and, through use and practice, is growing in his commitment to a Christian lifestyle.

I would like to consider "disciple-making" as a process—not only what one Christian can do in the life of another, but what the church can do for its individual members. When Jesus told his disciples to "go make disciples," He was speaking to them collectively, as a body. The only way a body can do anything is through the cooperative participation of its individual parts (1 Corinthians 12). I am not aware of any specific biblical command for one Christian, all by himself, to make a disciple, yet I believe that we should all be a part of the process.

Note some of the Greek words that the New Testament writers use to describe this process of disciple-making:

> Parakaleo: to exhort, encourage, comfort, console (found 105 times)
> Oikodomeo: to edify, build up (found thirty-seven times)
> Sterizo: to establish, conform, strengthen (found fourteen times)
> Katecheo: to instruct (found seven times)
> Didasko: to teach (found ninety-one times)
> Kerusso: to proclaim (found sixty times)

All of these go into the making of a disciple of Jesus Christ. It can be said that a disciple is the product of all the influences brought to bear upon a Christian's life, whether by a few or by many: preaching, teaching, instructing, establishing, confirming, strengthening, edifying, exhorting, modeling, and loving.

The church needs to understand the role of personal disciple-making and one-on-one ministry in the fulfillment of the Great Commission. How much of the disciple-making process can be carried out by one person in the life of another? One might conclude that most of it can be accomplished, if a strong one-on-one relationship can be established and sustained long enough. There is certainly biblical support for this concept of disciple-making. We need only to look at Jesus and His disciples. He ministered to the Twelve both individually and collectively, but He gave special attention to Peter, James, and John. While there may be no clear references in the New Testament to one-on-one disciple-making, the Paul-Timothy and Paul-Titus relationships, along with a few others, come close. Paul may have had this in mind when he wrote these words to Timothy: "And the things that you have heard from me among many witnesses, commit these to faithful men who will be able to teach others also" (2 Timothy 2:2).

Again, the church is under Christ's mandate to "go make disciples." What is your role in this process?

Man and His Work

. . . .

"The sun rises, then man goes out to his
work, to his labor until evening."
—Psalm 104:23

[This article is taken from my booklet *Life in the Marketplace*. Scripture quotations are taken from the *Holy Bible: New International Version*.]

We are often known by our vocations, as understood by such frequently asked questions as "What line of work are you in?" and "What do you do for a living?" People judge us on the basis of how we earn a living, sometimes drawing conclusions about such things as our education, income, lifestyle, and social status. Few things are as important as our work, for this is how we spend the majority of our waking hours, earn our income, and contribute to the society in which we live.

For Christians, however, there is another issue involved. God calls us to serve others and to minister to people, regardless of how we make a living. We, therefore, have a responsibility toward our coworkers and associates as well as toward others we encounter in the workplace.

Men often face tough questions when they come into a saving relationship with Jesus Christ, especially if they have a strong desire to minister to others. They may ask, "Should I view my work differently now that I am a follower of Christ? Can I still be content in my present career? Is it possible to integrate my work and ministry in such a way as to find fulfillment in both? Will God really use me at work to make a difference in people's lives, or should I consider going into 'the ministry'?"

Labor is an expression of God's grace, given to make our lives meaningful. Work is how God means for us to occupy our time in the perfection of His creation plan. When God created Adam, He "took the man and put him in the Garden of Eden to work it and take care of it" (Genesis 2:15). The author of Ecclesiastes wrote, "A man can do nothing better than to eat and drink and find satisfaction in his work. This too, I see, is from the hand of God" (Ecclesiastes 2:24). The apostle Paul, chosen by God to be a missionary to the Gentiles, was an evangelist and a church founder. He wrote much of the New Testament. Yet Paul was also a man who worked with his hands in a useful trade: "Because he was a tentmaker as they were, he stayed and worked with them" (Acts 18:3). In a letter to the Christians at Thessalonica, he wrote, "For you yourselves know how you ought to follow our example. We were not idle when we were with you, nor did we eat anyone's food without paying for it. On the contrary, we worked night and day, laboring and toiling so that we would not be a burden to any of you. We did this, not because we do not have the right to such help, but in order to make ourselves a model for you to follow. For even when we were with you, we gave you this rule: 'If a man will not work, he shall not eat'" (2 Thessalonians 3:7–10).

It is universally accepted that we must work in order to eat and acquire the other necessities of life. Jesus Himself was a working man, and He called twelve working men to be His first disciples. However, He did not demand that others who accepted Him give up their work, not even a notorious tax collector by the name of Zacchaeus (Luke 19:2). John the Baptist approved the work of tax collectors when he exhorted them to collect no more than was due. He also recognized the military profession by telling soldiers to be content with their pay (Luke 3:12–14).

According to the Bible, then, the first reason we work is because God commanded it. However, He did not command it just for the purpose of earning a living. God has already promised that He will provide us with the necessities of life. On the subject of food, drink, and clothing, Jesus said, "Your heavenly Father knows that you need them. But seek first his kingdom and his righteousness, and all these things will be given to you as well" (Matthew 6:32–33).

The second reason we work is to be in an environment where we can represent Jesus Christ. The workplace has been called the "nine-to-five window." It is not just a place to perform meaningful labor, but an environment for ministry. Not only are we to "work" as unto the Lord, we must also "minister" as unto the Lord.

Opportunities for ministry are as diverse as the marketplace itself. ("Marketplace" is used here to refer to the whole arena of jobs and places where people work.) Some workers—store clerks, for example—encounter many people each day, while others, such as farmers or construction workers, may come into contact with only a few.

Writing in defense of his ministry, Paul said, "We, however, will not boast beyond proper limits, but will confine our boasting to the field God has assigned to us" (2 Corinthians 10:13). God has assigned each of us a field of labor, a sphere of influence, which includes our work environment. As we minister in the marketplace, our ultimate goal is to help people come to know Jesus Christ as Savior and Lord and to help them grow in their relationship with Him.

God means for us to find contentment in our labor. To do this, we must view God as our boss and strive to please Him through our work. If we are business owners, we must relinquish ownership to God: "Whatever you do, work at it with all your heart, as working for the Lord, not for men, since you know that you will receive an inheritance from the Lord as a reward. It is the Lord Christ you are serving" (Colossians 3:23–24).

Confidence in Witnessing

"Now, Lord, look on their threats, and grant to your servants
that with all boldness they may speak Your word."
—Acts 4:29

[I wrote the following article while attending the Southern Baptist
Theological Seminary in Louisville, Kentucky. It appeared in the
September 1987 edition of *The Student* magazine, published by the
Sunday School Board of the Southern Baptist Convention.]

"I know I should witness more, but I just can't get up the nerve to do
it. I'm afraid I simply don't have what it takes to be a good witness."

Does this sound like you? If so, then believe me, you have plenty
of company, for most Christians do not witness like they should. I am
convinced, however, that this is not so much from a lack of knowledge
as from a lack of confidence.

Sharing our faith can be like pushing a stalled car. The hardest part
is getting started. It gets easier after that. This article is designed to help
you get started by showing you how to gain an opening to witness.

As you think about witnessing, remember Paul's words to Timothy:
"For God has not given us a spirit of fear, but of power and of love and
of a sound mind" (2 Timothy 1:7). Witnessing is simply sharing Christ
in the power of the Holy Spirit and leaving the results to God.

My first witnessing experiences were among college friends with
whom I was well acquainted. As I set out to share my faith with each of

them, I discovered that conversation among friends can easily be turned to spiritual things and be carried on sincerely and naturally.

Within such relationships, there is probably no better approach than to tell your friends that you want to share with them the most important thing in your life—your relationship with Jesus Christ. You'll be surprised to learn that people are often more willing to listen to the gospel than we are to share it.

But you cannot develop a relationship with everyone you meet. How, then, do you approach a stranger or casual acquaintance? The first step is to engage that person in conversation, and then you can turn toward spiritual things. Consider the following suggestions:

Look for a Sensitive Area

Many problems and circumstances that people face make them sensitive to the gospel. Loneliness, guilt, grief, fear, rejection, and other problems are sometimes easy to recognize and can provide the basis for a meaningful conversation. Also, just being friendly will occasionally lead a person to open up to you.

Jesus, knowing the guilt and loneliness of Zacchaeus, invited Himself to the publican's house. Shortly afterward, Zacchaeus trusted Him for salvation (Luke 19:1–10). Our Lord repeatedly dealt with people's problems as a means of reaching them spiritually.

Ask Someone a Favor

When a Samaritan woman came to draw water, Jesus said to her, "Give Me a drink" (John 4:7). He initiated a conversation by asking her a favor, and as a result, she, and many others, soon put their faith in Him. An unassuming question like "Can you tell me what time it is?" may be all it takes to initiate a conversation. You can offer to do someone a favor, such as giving him a ride home, creating an opportunity to witness.

Look Around

Seeing a student with a large, gold cross around his neck, I said, "I couldn't help noticing your cross. May I ask what the cross means to you?" On another occasion, I approached a student who was reading a book about natural science. "Do you believe in creation?" I asked. In both instances, I gained an opening to witness.

Be Creative

Wear a Christian pin and display some Christian posters in your room. Carry a Bible or New Testament, and read it openly. Pray over your meals in the cafeteria. Actions like these may prompt someone to approach you with a comment or question, which could open the door to witness.

After engaging a person in conversation, you must then direct your conversation toward spiritual things. One of the best ways to do this is to ask questions: "Are you a member of a church?" "Do you ever read the Bible?" "Do you believe in God?" "Are you a religious person?" Questions such as these not only help break the ice, but they also provide information about a person's spiritual background. Asking questions also makes witnessing easier by giving you control of the conversation.

Consider using the following sequence of questions: "Are you interested in spiritual things?" "Have you ever thought about becoming a Christian?" "How would you answer the question, 'What is a Christian?'"

Regardless of how these may be answered, you can respond by saying, "May I show you from the Bible just what I think it means to be a Christian?" This final question, however you arrive at it, will almost always give you an opening to share the gospel.

As a military pilot, I found that my greatest proficiency in flying came not while I was in the classroom or in the airplane with my instructor, but after I began to fly alone. My confidence increased steadily as I gained more and more experience in the air.

Personal witnessing is much the same. Once you have prepared adequately through study and prayer, the best way to gain confidence is by actually witnessing on your own.

Finally, witnessing will always require a certain amount of courage, so don't look for the perfect opportunity—it may never come. Instead, trust God to help you, for he said, "Therefore, go, and I will be with your mouth and teach you what you shall say" (Exodus 4:12).

The Great Commandment

"You shall love the Lord your God with all your heart,
with all your soul, and with all your strength."
—Deuteronomy 6:5

[This is "Part One" of a message delivered at the 2000 Fellowship of Christian Optometrists Annual Conference.]

One of my duties as a staff officer in the army was to process applications for hardship discharges and conscientious objector status. My superior directed me to some shelves that contained a dozen or more large binders.

"These are the Department of Defense Regulations," he said, pointing to one of the binders. He pointed to another one and said, "These are the Department of the Army Regulations." Then he showed me the Fort Leonard Wood Regulations, the US Army Training Center Regulations, the Brigade Regulations, and some other procedures and protocols. "Just familiarize yourself with all of these, and you'll have no problem doing this job. When the applications come through, check the regulations, write your reports, and send them up through channels."

Suppose all of those regulations could have been condensed into just a few simple rules, or, better yet, into a single statute or command. How much more focused the task would have been!

Jesus took all of the laws and commandments that God had given the Jewish people and summarized them as follows: "Love God and love your neighbor" (Mark 12:30–31). The apostle Paul streamlined the command even more: "For all the law is fulfilled in one word, even in this: 'You shall love your neighbor as yourself'" (Galatians 5:14). He understood that in order to truly love God, we must also love our neighbor; that genuine love for our neighbor is evidence of our love for God. The essential question is this: "What does it mean to love our neighbor?" If this is what we have to do to meet God's requirements, then it is imperative that we too understand what "loving our neighbor" is about!

Love meets needs in people's lives. Jesus told His disciples, "Do you not say, 'There are still four months and then comes the harvest'? Behold, I say to you, lift up your eyes and look at the fields, for they are already white for harvest!" (John 4:35). We observe an unending array of human needs: a man with a terminal illness; a woman suffering the pain of divorce or grieving over the death of a loved one; a man who has lost his job and is facing serious financial difficulties; a person living with discouragement or depression; a couple struggling with a problem teenager; an elderly woman with failing health and a fear of death; an accident victim living with pain; a single person dealing with loneliness; and people who just feel unloved or unappreciated.

God uses believers as His representatives, or agents, in sharing His love and compassion. People need a listening ear and words of kindness from someone who genuinely cares about them. Within every person is a desire to be wanted, needed, and fulfilled. Most important, though, is the need to know and experience the love of God and His power to change their lives. This comes only through a personal relationship with Jesus Christ.

Years ago, I traveled to Philadelphia, Pennsylvania, to attend an advanced optometry course. I was living in Louisville and wanted to ride a train, but there were no longer any trains running between Louisville and Philadelphia. I had to ride a bus to Indianapolis in order to catch a train to Philadelphia. Where there is no track, there can be no train. A train requires a track in order to go anywhere.

Similarly, love flows from one person to another through relationships, which provide opportunities to help people. Genuine friendliness, listening to their problems and concerns, displaying a sincere interest in them, and performing acts of kindness can lead to genuine, long-lasting relationships.

Christians are called to love believers and unbelievers alike. In the case of unbelievers, the goal is to gain opportunities to share Christ. What may begin with a casual conversation in the workplace could lead to a discussion about the Bible in the coffee shop or to sharing a word of testimony on the golf course. An intermediate goal should be to gain a person's confidence in order to engage him or her with the gospel. Sometimes this can take place very quickly. For example, a person receiving medical care from a missionary doctor may willingly listen to the message of Christ or accept a gospel tract. But apart from such ready-made situations, time and effort may be required to form the kind of relationships through which we can really love people and share the gospel with them.

Relationships are also helpful in demonstrating love to our brothers and sisters in Christ. Paul exhorted the Thessalonians to comfort and edify one another, to uphold the weak, to rejoice and pray for one another, and much more (1 Thessalonians 5:11–14). This is Christian love. Someone asked, "How do I know if I am loving people?" A wise counselor responded, "People will beat a path to your door, and your phone will not stop ringing when you genuinely love and care for them. They will witness and experience the love of God through you."

Jesus said, "Do not labor for the food which perishes, but for the food which endures to everlasting life, which the Son of Man will give you, because God the Father has set His seal on Him" (John 6:27). There are only two things that last forever: the Word of God and the souls of people. Loving God and loving people go together. We must impact people with the gospel. What, then, is the Great Commandment? It is to serve people as God gives us opportunities, to influence unbelievers toward salvation, and to encourage and assist fellow Christians in the path to spiritual maturity.

The Great Commission

• •

"Go therefore and make disciples of all the nations."
Matthew 28:18

[This is "Part Two" of a message delivered at the 2000 Fellowship of Christian Optometrists Annual Conference.]

In order to understand the Great Commission, let's consider an event that took place in 1776 during the American Revolution. Paul Revere's commanding officer called him in and said, "Paul, I want you to go through all the towns and villages and shout, 'The British are coming,' waking up all who are asleep, and stopping at all the taverns where people might be gathered." Now what was his command? Was it to go through the towns and villages? Yes. Was it to stop by the taverns where people might be found? Sure. Was his command to wake people up? Of course, but what was his primary command—the real purpose of his mission? What was Paul Revere sent to do? You guessed it. He was sent to shout, to cry as loud as he could, "The British are coming!"[7]

What are we commissioned to do? We are commissioned to make disciples: "Going therefore, make disciples—baptizing and teaching." The process involves baptizing and teaching, but the command is to make disciples. I believe that this began with God's command to Adam: "Be fruitful and multiply" (Genesis 1:28). He said it again when Noah and his family came off of the ark. Many years later, God promised Abraham: "I will make you exceedingly fruitful; and I will make nations

63

of you" (Genesis 17:6). It seems that multiplication has been on God's heart from the very beginning. The Great Commission involves that same principle of multiplication that God initiated back in Genesis. God is saying, "I want more just like you. I want every one of you to reproduce and multiply your life."

The Great Commission begins with evangelism: sharing the gospel with the goal of winning people to Jesus Christ. We can help carry out this command whether we are on some foreign mission field or in our regular place of work. We are involved in the work of evangelism any time we witness for Christ. But the Great Commission does not stop with evangelism—it includes helping new believers grow toward spiritual maturity through the process of disciple-making.

In Exodus, we read about Moses leading the Israelites out of Egypt after more than four-hundred years of slavery. Early in their journey, Moses ascended Mount Sinai to receive the Ten Commandments. During the forty days that he was on the mountain, the people grew restless and fell into idolatry. They built and worshiped a golden calf. The Bible says that they "cast off all restraint." When he came down from the mountain "Moses saw that the people were unrestrained (for Aaron had not restrained them, to their shame among their enemies)" (Exodus 32:25).

There is a city in South America that conducts an annual carnival where for one day each year, "anything goes." For that one day, the people just do whatever they want. They fill the streets of the city and celebrate—and running wild, without restraint. The word "carnival" comes from the word "carnal," which refers to "the flesh." The people just cast off all restraint and yield to the desires of the flesh. This seems to describe much of the world today—unrestrained and running wild.

The Bible says, "The boy Samuel ministered before the LORD under Eli. In those days the word of the Lord was rare; there were not many visions" (1 Samuel 3:1). In other words, the people of Israel rarely heard from God. The same word is used for "vision" in Proverbs 29:18: "Where there is no vision, the people cast off all restraint." The greatest challenge that we face as evangelical, mission-minded Christians is this:

the world is largely unrestrained, running wild and in need of the gospel of Jesus Christ. Christ is the only hope for the lost and dying masses. As with the Great Commandment, the Great Commission is about giving ourselves to people, that they might turn to God for salvation.

The Great Commitment

* *

"If anyone desires to come after Me, let him deny
himself and take up his cross, and follow Me."
—Matthew 16:24

[This is "Part Three" of a message delivered at the 2000 Fellowship of
Christian Optometrists Annual Conference.]

Jesus fed five thousand men, plus women and children, before preaching
His "Bread of Life" sermon. His words became so difficult to accept
that "many of His disciples went back and walked with Him no more.
Then Jesus said to the twelve, 'Do you also want to go away?' But Simon
Peter answered him, 'Lord, to whom shall we go? You have the words
of eternal life. Also we have come to believe and know that You are the
Christ, the Son of the living God'" (John 6:66–68). This is the "Great
Commitment."

Our commitment to Jesus Christ must not be too spontaneous,
emotional, or halfhearted: "Lord, I will follow you wherever you go, but
first let me graduate from optometry school." "Lord, I will follow you
wherever you go, but first let me pass my board exams; let me get my
practice established and my career underway; or let me get out of debt.
I will follow you after I get my life together!" We cannot follow Christ
on our own terms, but by wholehearted, unconditional commitment
to Him as the Lord of our lives. Jesus was speaking about this Great
Commitment when he said, "If anyone desires to come after Me, let

him deny himself, and take up his cross, and follow Me" (Matthew 16:24). The apostle Paul was referring to this Great Commitment when he wrote, "I have been crucified with Christ; it is no longer I who live, but Christ lives in me; and the life which I now live in the flesh I live by faith in the Son of God, who loved me and gave Himself for me" (Galatians 2:20).

Jehu said, "Come with me, and see my zeal for the LORD" (2 Kings 10:16). As a new Christian, I was enthusiastic about sharing my newly discovered faith in Jesus Christ. My goal at that time was to verbally witness to each of the twenty students in my optometry class. (Some were already Christians.) Later, I realized that I had set my sights too short; my goal should have been to witness to every student in the school as well as the faculty.

Once, after I had spoken at a church near Birmingham, my photograph and an article about the event appeared in a local newspaper. The next morning, my clinical instructor said wryly, "Segree, I didn't know that you were a man of the cloth." I did not consider myself "a man of the cloth," but the occasion did give me an opportunity to witness. Later, I came to understand that God's plan is for *every* believer to present a positive witness for Jesus Christ in the workplace.

May we never have to say, "God, what have I done with my life? I have devoted my life to the wrong things: the pursuit of wealth, materialism, pleasure, power, and the like." Instead, may we be led by these words of Jesus: "Do not labor for the food which perishes, but for the food which endures to everlasting life" (John 6:27).

God spoke through the prophet Isaiah: "Fear not, for I have redeemed you; I have summoned you by name; you are Mine… since you are precious and honored in My sight, and because I love you, I will give men in exchange for you, and people in exchange for your life" (Isaiah 43:1, 4). This is a promise every believer can claim. "God, give people for my life. Let me exchange my life for people. Let me invest in people"—this is the spirit of the Great Commandment, the Great Commission, and the Great Commitment.

The People Business

[This article is taken from my booklet *Life in the Marketplace*. Scripture quotations are taken from the *Holy Bible: New International Version*.]

Missionary life in Calcutta, India, would be quite different from that in inner city Chicago, La Paz, Bolivia, or the jungles of Papua, New Guinea. Missionaries have to be uniquely qualified to serve in such diverse settings around the world. This diversity can be seen in the environment, climate, culture, race, language, religion, and other regional characteristics.

There is also great diversity in the mission field known as "the marketplace." Work environments differ in countless ways: a corporate executive's office, a factory, a construction site, a hospital, an elementary school, a department store, or a restaurant. For those whose jobs bring them into contact with the public, there are frequent encounters with new people, while others associate with the same people every day. In some situations, workers can talk freely, yet in others, this type of interaction is almost impossible. Some people spend most of the workday alone, while others are never alone. Regardless of our particular work environment, as Christians, we are, in a sense, in the same business— the people business.

Ministry may be defined as "specialized, concentrated activities or actions carried out in the name of Jesus Christ by groups or individuals utilizing God-given gifts, natural talents, or acquired skills to (a) serve people in need; (b) influence unbelievers toward salvation; and (c) encourage Christians toward spiritual maturity."[8] Our methods and techniques for ministry may vary, yet certain principles apply, no matter what our work environment might be.

Jesus said, "You are the salt of the earth...You are the light of the world" (Matthew 5:13–14). Jesus used salt and light to illustrate the effect that our lives should have upon other people. Just as salt is an appetizer, the quality of our lives should be appealing to those who observe us. We should strive to be above reproach in our speech, attitudes, and actions: "As a prisoner for the Lord, then, I urge you to live a life worthy of the calling you have received" (Ephesians 4:1). In the same way that light shines from a lamp, the light and life of Jesus Christ must shine forth from us. People are quick to recognize the difference between what we say and what we do. If we act one way and talk another, people will always assume that the actions represent the real truth about us. Another reason that "living the life" is so important is that disobedience, even the smallest sin, grieves God, quenches the Spirit, and deprives us of God's power to work. As it says in the Bible, "And do not grieve the Holy Spirit of God" (Ephesians. 4:30) and "Do not put out the Spirit's fire" (1 Thessalonians 5:19).

Christ uses believers as his representatives, or agents, in sharing His love, compassion, and wisdom. Believers and unbelievers alike should be the objects of Christian ministry. We must be prepared to share the gospel with people who have not heard or understood it, yet also be ready to serve and encourage our brothers and sisters in Christ. Paul exhorted the Thessalonians to comfort and edify one another, to uphold the weak, to rejoice and pray for one another, and much more (1 Thessalonians 5:11–14).

We can minister most effectively through human relationships: "So, affectionately longing for you, we were well pleased to impart to you not only the gospel of God, but also our own lives, because you had become dear to us" (1 Thessalonians 2:8 NKJV). Inside every person, there is a desire to be wanted, needed, and fulfilled. A personal relationship with Jesus Christ is what truly satisfies these deep longings. Our ultimate goal in ministry is to help people come to know Christ and grow in their relationship with Him.

People must hear about Christ in order to believe in Him: "How, then, can they call on the one they have not believed in? And how can they believe in the one of whom they have not heard? And how can they hear without someone preaching to them?" (Romans 10:14). "Consequently, faith comes from hearing the message, and the message is heard through the word of Christ" (Romans 10:17).

There are many ways by which a person can be exposed to the gospel: from the words of a preacher or Bible teacher; by reading the Bible or an evangelistic gospel tract; by listening to someone share how he or she got saved; or by attending a Christian musical or dramatic event. In any case, for .people to be saved, they must first understand the gospel message. We must develop relationships while living lives that conform to biblical standards, but unless we tell people how they can know Christ, nobody will be saved. Nobody ever went to heaven simply by observing the exemplary life of some Christian friend or acquaintance. There must also have been a clear communication of the gospel.

After making a decision to accept Christ, a man was congratulated by his boss. "Are you a Christian?" the employee asked.

"Oh, yes," replied the senior man. "I've been a Christian for many years."

"I have always known you to be a fair, considerate, and honest man," said the other. "If you had told me about Christ, I might have accepted Him long ago."

We will probably never know how many people have been lost to the kingdom of God because we failed to tell them about our own relationship with Christ and about how they, too, could have eternal life.

Consider your own work environment. You can take a mental survey of your coworkers, noting your impression as to those who seem to be Christians and others who do not. Then pray about how you can best approach them, asking God to show you how to encourage the believers and how to tell the unbelievers about Jesus.

Ministry begins when we identify a need in someone's life and initiate some course of action. More often than not, this action involves talking to the person and then determining how we can help. If the ministry involves sharing the gospel, there may be some anxiety or fear to overcome. This usually disappears once we begin to talk about Christ and spiritual things.

Start by listening and looking for some common ground for interaction. Focus on a person's interests or on some obvious area of need. Ask key questions to turn the conversation toward God and Jesus Christ, such as, "Are you interested in spiritual things?" "Do you believe in God?" "Do you attend church?" and "Do you ever read the Bible?" Be a little bold in your effort to connect on spiritual matters. Give the person an appropriate gospel tract or contemporary translation of the New Testament. Ask, "How can I pray for you?" You may be able to encourage him or her right then and there, to share a word of testimony, or to invite the person to Bible study or church. In other instances, you will need to follow up at some more opportune time. But remember—ministry to unbelievers should always have as one of its objectives a clear presentation of the gospel of Jesus Christ.

Support your ministry with prayer: "Devote yourselves to prayer, being watchful and thankful. And pray for us, too, that God may open a door for our message, so that we may proclaim the mystery of Christ, for which I am in chains" (Colossians 4:2–3). As a young Christian, Dawson Trotman, founder of The Navigators, would often begin his day with this simple prayer: "Lord, we're just reporting for duty. We don't know who we'll meet today or what their need will be, but give us the right word for them." [9]

Try starting each day with a prayer such as this: "Heavenly Father, I am going into my mission field today, looking for opportunities to minister to people in the name of Jesus Christ. Grant me the discernment to recognize these opportunities, the wisdom to respond to them properly, and the faith to trust You to work in the lives of people I meet. Let me be salt and light so that they might be drawn to Christ through my life. Cause me to speak the right words at the right time and in the right way. In Jesus' name I pray. Amen."

SECTION III

Letters

An Exciting Life

. . . .

"For our citizenship is in heaven, from which we also eagerly
wait for the Savior, the Lord Jesus Christ."
—Philippians 3:20

["How would you men like to make one-fifth of what you made for
many years, beginning tomorrow? It's exciting!" said Howard Borland,
speaking to the Cahaba Heights Baptist Church in Birmingham on
January 26, 1975. This gifted man of God led more people to Christ
than anyone I have ever known. Years earlier, he had given up his
business as a certified public accountant in order to devote his time
fully to the ministry. His excitement was contagious. Even today, I am
encouraged when I reflect upon some of the letters and conversations
we had in the early years of my Christian life.]

January 13, 1981

Dear Joe,

It would be a joy to sit down with you and discuss how God led me
out of my business, along with how he is dealing with you. Of course
God deals differently with each person, but when we know we are ready
to move away from worldly occupations, we always have one thing in
common—a quiet, peaceful inner assurance from the Holy Spirit that
this is the way in which we should walk. The important thing is to
have the Lord Jesus Christ in control of our lives. When we are willing

to do anything he wants, we will have this peace, and he will show us clearly the path we should take. It would be wonderful to visit with you in person. Dixie and I will continue to pray about God's leading in your life.

We are staying quite busy with a diversified ministry. We just praise God for the fact that he uses frail sinners. In the last two or three years, we have seen a lot of bread cast on the waters that has come back manyfold. People have been genuinely saved, taught the Word, and called into the ministry to serve in many different ways to the glory of God.

Presently, I am teaching four classes a week; Dixie is teaching two. We still do some telephone evangelism and are about to go to Michigan for an eight-day period. Also, we are conducting some financial seminars. Through my experience as a CPA, God has given us some informative material to help people with their finances. We are also doing quite a bit of counseling these days. The Birmingham Police Department and the county Sheriff's Department have called upon us to aid their Christian workers in many areas. This is a very vital and exciting field. God has richly blessed us in every possible way.

Thank you for your very gracious letter. I prayed about the content of my previous letter to you and hope it didn't sound too harsh, wouldn't register adversely, and that it was of the Lord. In any event, you have accepted it in a sweet way, and if the advice was beneficial, we praise the Lord. God is doing a great work among young couples today. How critical it is to get our personal and family lives in order and then take a bold stand where people do mean business about Christ.

May God really bless you physically, socially, financially, and, most of all, spiritually.

In Christ,
Howard

No Unrealistic Expectations

"Then after some days Paul said to Barnabas, 'Let us now
go back and visit our brethren in every city where we have
preached the word of the Lord, and see how they are doing.'"
Acts 15:36

[Walter Henrichsen, author of the classic *Disciples Are Made, Not Born*
and other books, wrote the following letter in response to my inquiry
regarding an issue of ministry with fellow optometrists. "Jim" refers to
Jim Webster, now with the Lord in heaven, a mutual brother in the Lord
and my spiritual mentor for more than twenty-five years.]

December 2, 1999

Dear Joe,

I have in front of me your good letter of some weeks ago. I apologize
for being tardy in getting back to you, but have been on the road
a great deal these past days. Jim is a great brother, and I know you
would be richly blessed by joining The Navigators in their Business and
Professional ministry.

You asked for my input regarding integrating your ministry with
optometrists "from afar." I am not sure how much help I can give you
in this regard, but let me ramble somewhat.

It seems that your objective must be to help men become all they
feel God wants them to be. As you minister from afar, you are not going

to be able to take them by the hand and lead them day by day, month in, and month out. For this reason, you are going to need a key man (or spark plug) in each geographical locale you seek to impact. This man on the scene must be a self-starter, sustaining himself with little or no outside help. These kinds of men are hard to find. They are a gift from God.

It is imperative in ministering to them that you do not establish any unrealistic expectations. Resist the temptation to develop hoops through which they must jump. You can challenge them, but if they don't see the value, then you can take them no further. Leveraging them will not help.

Although it is possible to minister from afar, you still need personal contact, which means being on the road a great deal. Most of my ministry for the last twenty-five years has entailed heavy travel. I suggest that it is a price you have to pay if you are going to pull it off.

Technology is on our side, and we are rapidly moving to the place where video teleconferencing will be both feasible and economical. That will greatly assist in staying in touch.

Finally, it seems to me that your primary objective further involves helping these men develop the mind of Christ. There is no short cut to this, as I tried to point out in my first day of the devotional.[10] It requires years of hard work. There are little coveys of men across the country with whom I am in touch that have memorized books like Romans, Hebrews, 1 and 2 Corinthians, thus spending a minimum of twenty hours per chapter in preparation prior to our meeting together to study it. These are the kind of men who "become the foundation of many generations."

Wishing you well, I am

Your Brother in Christ,
Walt

Be Encouraged

* *

"But encourage one another daily."
—Hebrews 3:13

[I received the following letter from my friend R. T. Spivey at a time when I was undergoing a prolonged health problem.]

March 18, 2005

Dear Joe,

Good morning to you! I have prayed for the King of Heaven to intervene and heal.

I know that you and Alma have a heart for God and that you are seeking to disciple and multiply your lives through others. Give glory to Jesus, the resurrected Lamb, who sits upon the throne.

I have found an intriguing book: *The Holiest of All* by Andrew Murray. This book has helped me and has been a virtual spiritual oasis during my many trials of physical infirmity. I may not have told you, but I have broken over twenty bones in my body and have an ongoing bout with pain each day. But God's grace and strength are sufficient. I do not share this to "one up on you," but simply to let you know that I understand some of what you are going through. Just this morning I read Isaiah 32:1–8 in my quiet time, and it seemed to speak to me of you.

The time you spent with me in Brookhaven[11]was of infinite worth. I know that nothing will ever take away or change the work of faith and labor of love that you did there. You demonstrated and shared with me the very presence of the resurrected Christ, who is alive and well and lives forevermore!

The older I get, the more I realize that we are His treasure. We are a special gift from the Father to the Son (John 6:37). May our gracious God touch and heal you speedily, but if your sickness is "for the glory of God," He will give you the grace to overcome. Our Heavenly Father may instead choose to remove your infirmities little at a time, or however He sees fit.

Bless you brother. Stay in touch.

By His Eternal Love,
R. T.
Jude 24–25

Another View of God's Love

❖ • ❖ • ❖ • ❖ • ❖ • ❖ • ❖ • ❖ • ❖ • ❖ • ❖ • ❖ • ❖ • ❖ • ❖ • ❖ • ❖ • ❖ • ❖

"For God so loved the world that He gave His only begotten Son,
that whoever believes in Him should not perish
but have everlasting life."
—John 3:16

[I wrote the following letter to my brother to present some new thoughts about God's love.]

December 14, 2000

Dear John,

In a conversation with Angela a few days ago, I made the comment that "God loves all people." She replied, "Where in the Bible does it say that, Dad?" I came back with, "Well, uh, uh, uh?" "Show me the verse," she said. "I'll have to get back with you on this one," I responded because all I could come up with was John 3:16. Right away, I began to search the Bible for those "other" verses that speak of God's love for the whole world.

Does God love all people? What does the Bible say? John 3:16 says "yes," if "the world" refers to all people. First Timothy 2:4 and 2 Peter 3:9 imply "yes." Matthew 28:19 and other Great Commission verses certainly suggest so. The nature and activity of God revealed in Scripture clearly reflect His love for all people, as do the life, ministry, and death of Jesus Christ.

But where does the Bible actually *say* that God loves everybody, the heathen included? I have come to the conclusion that it just does not do so. The Bible is replete with expressions of God's love for Israel and for the Church. Why does it not say that God loves all people, even those who do not accept Him, those who do not become a part of His family of believers? A friend was quick to remind me, however, that God does not need to say something more than once for it to be true!

God's love for Israel can be seen in such passages as Deuteronomy 4:37; 23:5; 33:3; Psalm 47:4; 78:68; Isaiah 43:4; Jeremiah 31:3; and the Song of Solomon. Regarding the Church, consider John 16:27; Romans 1:7; 5:8; 8:37-39; 2 Thessalonians 2:16; and 1 John 4:9–11.

In the Bible, God has revealed Himself and His plan for the redemption of the human race. Since this includes believers from both Israel and the Church, perhaps there is no reason for God to say much about His love for those who will ultimately reject Him. Yet we do know from 2 Peter 3:9 that "God is not willing that any should perish but that all should come to repentance."

I am not claiming to have uncovered any new revelation or theological truth, but the fact remains that I have found no verse, other than John 3:16, that specifically states that God loves all people. It is a good thing to be challenged spiritually and biblically by one's own child.

What do you think?

Love,
Joe

Opportunities

. . . .

"For a great and effective door has opened to me."
—1 Corinthians 16:9

[I wrote the following letter to the Board of Directors of the Fellowship of Christian Optometrists.]

December 13, 1994

Dear Colleagues,

The 1994 FCO Conference has come and gone. What a great weekend! I would like to share with you my thoughts of what an FCO conference is all about. It can be expressed most appropriately, perhaps, by the word "opportunity."

An FCO conference is an opportunity to meet Christian optometrists and students from all across America and to begin new, meaningful, and lasting relationships. It is an occasion to learn how to become involved in eye care missions, whether in one's usual place of practice or on some foreign mission field.

An FCO conference offers excellent continuing education presented by Christian optometrists and a chance to dialogue with like-minded Christian colleagues. It may even be an opportunity for discovering God's direction for your life or career. My only regret is that the weekend passes so quickly. The opportunities are there and then they are gone.

Life is much the same. We have a lifetime of opportunities and then they are gone. One of the wonderful things about being a follower of Jesus Christ is that we can know the real meaning and purpose of life and thus recognize those things that really matter.

Jesus said, "A new commandment I give to you, that you love one another" (John 13:34) and "You shall love your neighbor as yourself" (Matthew 22:39). God wants us to spend our lives loving and helping others, and has provided us with unlimited opportunities to do just that. People are what really matter.

When the big conference of life is over, what will matter will be how we used the opportunities God gave us: to share Christ with others, to help meet human needs in Jesus' name, to use our gifts and abilities—indeed to use our lives for the glory of God. Let us redeem the time and make the most of every opportunity.

Thank you for your willingness to stand up and be counted as a Christian optometrist.

Your Brother in Christ,
Joe

Our Greatest Bond

* *

"Now you are the body of Christ, and members individually."
—1 Corinthians 12:27

[I wrote the following letter to the Board of Directors of the Fellowship of Christian Optometrists.]

January 13, 1995

Dear Colleagues,

Next month, I will begin a Sunday morning teaching ministry in a chapel at Fort Knox. This ministry is sponsored by The Navigators and has been around for several years. Attendance is voluntary. I will be working with young men assigned to Fort Knox for thirteen weeks of basic and advanced individual training. I am excited about this opportunity and am praying that God will use it to make a real difference in the lives of many young men.

These men may never know that I am an optometrist. They will not know about FCO, annual conferences, optometric missions, or student chapters. They won't hear about Christian Vision or New Vision Ministries.

Likewise, I'm sure that many to whom you minister may never know that you are an optometrist. Yet we do not minister because we are members of FCO, but because we are members of God's family— because we are Christians.

I thank God for FCO and for the unique opportunities it provides for ministering to people, but it is not our only area of ministry. Our greatest contribution to the kingdom of God may come altogether apart from our roles as Christian optometrists or our involvement with an organization called the Fellowship of Christian Optometrists.

Regardless of what we are doing in our churches and communities or how we are serving God through FCO, we remain committed to the common purpose of leading people to the Lord Jesus Christ. This is our greatest bond as Christian optometrists.

Let us thank God for whatever opportunities He provides for ministry and service through FCO, and then let us continue to minister in other ways, knowing that this too is part of our calling as Christian optometrists.

May we be more available than ever to serve the Lord Jesus Christ!

Your Brother in Christ,
Joe

A Babe Was Born

. . . .

"For there is born to you this day in the city of David
a Savior, who is Christ the Lord."
—Luke 2:11

[I had little opportunity to spend time with Grandmother Segree during my growing up years. My family lived a long distance away, so we saw my father's parents only once every two or three years. I fondly remember that when I was twelve years old, she tried to teach me how to read the Gospel of John in Spanish. Grandmother taught school for many years and was a prolific writer. Her writings were mostly religious and inspirational, including a long-running newspaper column, "The Book."

Nellie Segree was a woman of great faith, one who believed the Bible and held firmly to the promises of God. Her confidence in the faithfulness of God can be seen on every page of her writings. Her belief in heaven was unshakable. She wanted everyone to know about and experience it personally. Nellie never sought praise for her writings. To her, Christ alone is worthy of our praise and adulation.

The article that follows, though not a letter, is included in this section because of its personal nature. Grandmother sent this pamphlet to Alma and me on one of our first Christmases together.]

On December 25, we celebrate the birth of a child who was born nearly two thousand years ago. He was born in a stable because there was no room in the inn. Some knew of the nature of this child before His birth or while He was still an infant: Mary, Joseph, Elisabeth, the shepherds, the wise men, Simeon, Anna, and later, John the Baptist.

When He reached the age of thirty and began His ministry, few remembered that His birth had been announced by angels, by shepherds, by the stars, and by direct revelation. Probably those still living had lost their faith in what they had seen or heard—at least some had. It is also possible that many did not hear of Jesus' ministry. Transportation and communication were very slow in those days. Remember, too, that they were looking for a king to deliver them from their Roman rulers, so they paid little attention to rumors of a humble carpenter, even when miraculous things were told of Him.

To fully appreciate the babe of Bethlehem, you should know Him. Study His life and evaluate your own life in the light of His teaching. Use the Sermon on the Mount (Matthew 5–7) as a yardstick. This is bound to make you humble, and humility is a must if you would know Him.

Unless He dwells within your heart, you cannot truly celebrate His birth. He is the Savior of the world, the way to everlasting glory, our Lord and Friend. He should command our love, respect, and obedience through time and eternity.

—Nellie T. Segree

Love,
Grandmother

SECTION IV
Tracts

Our Eyes: A Christian Perspective

* *

Our eyes…

are priceless.

Without them, we would live in a different world, for our greatest awareness of the things around us comes through our eyes.

are miraculous.

The phenomenon of sight can be explained in no other way. Only God could have created these organs of sight and given us the gift of vision.

are part of our bodies.

As such, they change as we grow. As age makes its marks upon our bodies, unfortunately, it does not exclude our eyes. Eventually, our vision begins to grow dim.

While science continues to make new discoveries about the eyes and vision, it still cannot restore eyesight that has been lost. *But one day, perfect vision will be restored unto all people!* This truth cannot be found in medical and scientific literature, but it has been revealed to us through the greatest book of all—the Bible.

"In that day… the eyes of the blind shall see out of obscurity and out of darkness" (Isaiah 29:18).

What is it that we shall see in that day? The Bible says that it is the Son of God, the Lord Jesus Christ whom we shall all see with perfect vision.

"Your eyes will see the King in His beauty" (Isaiah 33:17).

The future coming of Jesus Christ, of which the Bible speaks so often, is just as certain as His first coming two thousand years ago. We shall all see the glory of His coming.

"This same Jesus, who was taken up from you into heaven, will so come in like manner as you saw Him go into heaven" (Acts 1:11)

"Behold, He is coming with the clouds, and every eye will see Him, even those who pierced Him" (Revelation 1:7).

Not only will every eye see Him, but:

"At the name of Jesus every knee should bow… and every tongue should confess that Jesus Christ is Lord, to the glory of God the Father" (Philippians 2:10–11).

Yet while all humankind will one day see Him, bow down to Him, and confess that He is Lord, only those who have individually trusted Christ will be saved.

"Nor is there salvation in any other, for there is no other name under heaven given among men by which we must be saved" (Acts 4:12).

My friend, although your natural vision may be perfect, you may still be suffering from spiritual blindness. May your spiritual eyes now be opened to God's wonderful plan of salvation!

You must confess that you are a sinner separated from God.

"For there is not a just man on earth who does good and does not sin" (Ecclesiastes 7:20).

"For all have sinned and fall short of the glory of God" (Romans 3:23).

"Your iniquities have separated you from your God; and your sins have hidden His face from you" (Isaiah 59:2).

You cannot reach God by your own effort, but there is a solution. There is a way to come to God!

"God demonstrates His own love toward us, in that while we were still sinners, Christ died for us" (Romans 5:8).

"For God so loved the world that He gave His only begotten Son, that whosoever believes in Him should not perish but have everlasting life" (John 3:16).

You can reach God only by coming through Jesus Christ. Jesus said, "I am the way, the truth and the life. No one comes to the Father except through Me" (John 14:6).

You must repent and receive Christ.

To repent is to turn from your sins and be willing to change your way of living. You cannot do this completely on your own, but God will help you if you ask him.

"Unless you repent you will all likewise perish" (Luke 13:3).

Christ is alive! You must *individually* invite Him into your life and ask Him to forgive you of your sins and give you the gift of eternal life.

"For the wages of sin is death, but the gift of God is eternal life in Christ Jesus our Lord" (Romans 6:23).

Jesus said, "Behold I stand at the door and knock. If anyone hears My voice and opens the door, I will come in to him and dine with him, and he with Me" (Revelation 3:20).

"But as many as received Him, to them He gave the right to become children of God, to those who believe in His name" (John 1:12).

Christ wants you to let Him come into your life! You can receive Christ right now through prayer.

Just pray this prayer sincerely, and Christ will come into your life, as He has promised:

"Lord Jesus, I am a sinner, and I cannot save myself. I believe that You died on the cross for my sins. Please forgive me and come into my life as Savior and Lord. Give me the gift of eternal life and make me the kind of person You want me to be."

If you invited Jesus Christ into your life, the Bible says that you now have eternal life.

"And this is the testimony: that God has given us eternal life, and this life is in His Son. He who has the Son has life; he who does not have the Son of God does not have life" (1 John 5:11–12).

Now that you have trusted Christ, do not rely upon your feelings, but upon the trustworthiness of the Bible, God's Word. As you read the Bible, you will gain greater and greater assurance and understanding of your new relationship with God.

The Witness of the Heavens

Since the beginning of time, people have gazed at the stars with a sense of awe over their beauty and majesty. If you get away from the city lights on a clear night and look up to the sky, you might see well over one thousand stars. With a good amateur telescope, the number will be significantly greater. Visit an observatory and look through one of the giant telescopes, and you will see why the word "astronomical" is used to describe things of enormous size.

The galaxy in which our solar system is located contains over 100 billion stars, and there are billions of galaxies in the universe. (It is difficult, if not impossible, to discuss the vastness of the universe without using scientific terminology, so bear with me as we consider the magnitude of the heavens.) Astronomers have statistically estimated that there are about 10^{25} stars (that is, 10 million, billion billions) in the known universe. If a person could count even as many as twenty numbers per second, it would still take at least 100 million, billion years to count up to 10^{25}.

The extent of the universe is truly incomprehensible! Light travels at a speed of 186,000 miles per second—about six trillion miles per year. This "light-year" is a convenient measure of distance in space. Light from the sun, some 93 million miles away, takes about eight minutes to reach earth, while the light from Alpha Centauri, the closest star to earth at 24.2 trillion miles, makes the trip in about 4.2 years. The farthest distance measurable with the best modern telescope is about 333 light-years, yet within our own galaxy, most stars are even farther away than this. What a small bit of space we actually see in the night sky. As the Bible says, "Indeed these are the mere edges of His ways" (Job 26:14).

Consider our own solar system, made up of the sun, eight planets, some seventy moons, and innumerable asteroids, comets, and other interplanetary debris. Its boundaries are a mere 3.7 billion miles apart (the distance from the sun to Pluto at its farthest point in orbit). The arrangement, alignment, motion, speed, size, mass, and orbital pattern of these heavenly bodies have been the subject of human study for hundreds, if not thousands, of years. Their precision and orderliness, not to mention the myriad of stars in the heavens, staggers the imagination and leads any rational person to ask, "Where did the universe come from? Was it created, has it always existed, or did it just happen? If there is a Creator, what is He like?"

For centuries, priests and philosophers have studied cosmology: the nature, structure, origin, and end of the universe. In the twentieth century, astronomers joined their ranks, and as a result, many in the scientific (and nonscientific) world now believe that the stars, along with everything else in the universe, are hurling away from one another at enormous speeds. The reason? The universe exploded with a "big bang" some 15 billion years ago! This theory, proposed in the 1940s, suggests that the universe began as an unimaginably dense point that exploded and has been expanding ever since, cooling and coalescing into ever more organized states of matter. Where did this dense, point-like mass come from? No answer has been given. Another proposal followed, known as the "Steady State Theory," that the universe had no beginning and will have no end. Of these, and perhaps some lesser known theories, the Big Bang won out. This seems to be the best that man, by his own wisdom, can do to explain the origin of things!

For a Christian, however, there is a perfectly acceptable explanation for the origin of the universe—one that does not leave unanswered the ultimate question of how it began: "In the beginning God created the heavens and the earth" (Genesis 1:1). In addition, "By the word of the LORD the heavens were made, and all the host of them by the breath of His mouth" (Psalm 33:6).

Just as God is infinite, the number of stars may also be infinite, innumerable, and without end. One look into the night sky should cause us to rejoice at the power and majesty of the Creator! The Bible attests to this: "The heavens declare the glory of God" (Psalm 19:1), "Is not God in the height of heaven? And see the highest stars, how lofty they are!" (Job 22:12), and "Lift up your eyes on high, and see who has created these things, who brings out their host by number; He calls them all by name, by the greatness of His might and the strength of His power; not one is missing" (Isaiah 40:26).

As for the origin of the hosts of heaven, the earth was created first, then the sun and moon to rule the day and night, then finally, the stars: "I have made the earth, and created man on it. I—My hands—stretched out the heavens, and all of their host I have commanded" (Isaiah 45:12). To those who doubt these truths, God says, "For as the heavens are higher than the earth, so are My ways higher than your ways, and My thoughts than your thoughts" (Isaiah 55:9). As we think about the vastness of space and the splendor of a star-filled sky, is there any wonder that the psalmist should write, "When I consider Your heavens, the work of Your fingers, the moon and the stars which You have ordained, what is man that You are mindful of him?" (Psalm 8:3–4). From these and many other passages of Scripture, we see that the biblical writers, by the inspiration of the Spirit of God, attributed the origin of the heavens to the one and only God—the God of the Bible.

While proponents of the Big Bang Theory must acknowledge its essential flaw—that it does not explain the origin of this "unimaginably dense point" from which they claim that all things have come—they nevertheless seem to reject the notion that one can know anything by faith. The Bible says, "But without faith it is impossible to please Him, for He who comes to God must believe that He is, and that He is a rewarder of those who diligently seek Him" (Hebrews 11:6).

One cannot read the Bible and not be confronted with its ultimate theme and message: God's redemption of the human race through his Son Jesus Christ. The God that made the stars and calls them all "by name" entered the world as an infant child, born of a virgin in the humblest of surroundings. His advent that first Christmas was marked by an extraordinary star and heralded by angels. Thirty-three years later, He was crucified by Roman soldiers, but on the third day, He arose from the grave, triumphing over death and fulfilling God's plan for the salvation of all who would receive Him. The Bible says, "For all have sinned and fall short of the glory of God" (Romans 3:23) and "But as many as received Him, to them He gave the right to become children of God, to those who believe in His name" (John 1:12).

Dear friend, the next time you gaze into the heavens, be assured that you are witnessing the handiwork of God—the God who loved you so much "that He gave His only begotten Son, that whoever believes in Him should not perish but have eternal life" (John 3:16). If you have not taken that step of faith by which you can enter into a saving relationship with the God and Creator of the universe, you can do so right now. Pray this prayer sincerely, and Jesus Christ will come into your life: "Lord Jesus, Creator of heaven and earth, I am a sinner, and I cannot save myself. I believe that you died on the cross for my sins and were raised from the dead. Please forgive me, come into my life as Savior and Lord, and give me the gift of eternal life."

Making Right Choices

Biblical Guidelines

The Bible says, "I will instruct you and teach you in the way you should go; I will guide you with My eye" (Psalm 32:8). As Christians, we may believe and claim this promise from the Bible, but how can we be sure that God is leading us when we face difficult choices? This tract presents certain guidelines for recognizing God's direction in our lives. The knowledge and application of these guidelines will enable us to make wise decisions. The Bible says, "Do not be conformed to this world, but be transformed by the renewing of your mind, that you may prove what is that good and acceptable and perfect will of God" (Romans 12:2). The "renewing of your mind" involves certain steps that are essential to discerning God's will.

a. *You Must Be Saved.* The first step toward knowing the will of God is to accept Jesus Christ as your Savior. God will show the way to those who trust and obey Him. His will for every person is, first and foremost, to repent and believe the gospel. "For the Son of Man has come to seek and to save that which was lost" (Luke 19:10).

b. *You Must Be Searching.* While much of God's sovereign plan for the universe and the human race is hidden from us, His moral will has been revealed through the Scriptures. Although God can work in our lives however He chooses, He speaks to us primarily through the Bible. You must look to the Scriptures for God's direction. "I delight to do your will, O my God, and Your law is within my heart" (Psalm 40:8).

c. *You Must Be Separated.* Sin and undue involvement in the things of the world cloud our minds and keep us from discerning God's guidance. It is imperative that you separate yourself from ungodly and evil practices and influences. "Blessed are the pure in heart, for they shall see God" (Matthew 5:8).

d. *You Must Be Surrendered.* You must yield yourself completely to God, telling him that you are fully His and that you will do anything He asks. "Present your bodies a living sacrifice holy, acceptable to God, which is your reasonable service" (Romans 12:1).

Consider the following biblical guidelines for discerning God's leading:

1. *First, be willing to do what God wants you to do.* You must walk by faith, trusting God to guide you according to His plan for your life. If you say, "Lord, show me what You want me to do," but think, "then I will decide whether or not to do it," the Bible calls you "double-minded" and "unstable" (James 1:5–8). Do not expect guidance from God unless you are willing to obey.

2. *Read and study the Bible.* God may speak to you through your daily devotional reading as well as through passages of Scripture relevant to the issue you are facing. But you must be "rightly dividing the word of truth" (2 Timothy 2:15), avoiding the tendency to let it say what you want to hear. As you meditate upon the Scriptures, you may find the Holy Spirit gently nudging you in a particular direction.

3. *Do not seek God's will concerning things commanded or forbidden in the Scriptures.* The Bible reveals the express will of God and often requires little or no clarification. What the Bible commands, you are to obey; what it forbids, you must not do.

"Forever, O LORD, Your word is settled in heaven" (Psalm 119:89).

4. *Consider the desires of your heart, along with your natural gifts and abilities.* God did not give you these gifts and not intend for you to use them. The desires of your heart, if they honor God and are not contrary to the Scriptures, provide guidance for most situations you face. God gives you freedom of choice in most of life's decisions. As the Bible says, "Delight yourself also in the Lord, and He shall give you the desires of your heart" (Psalm 37:4).

5. *Ask God to guide you and give you wisdom for making the right choice.* God acts in response to prayer. "If any of you lacks wisdom, let him ask of God, who gives to all liberally" (James 1:5).

6. *Examine your conscience in relation to this course of action.* What are your motives? Are you being honest with God and with yourself? Are you truly seeking God's will or just looking for Him to sanction your will? "O LORD, You have searched me and known me... You understand my thought afar off" (Psalm 139:1–2).

7. *Use common sense.* Does the course of action you are considering seem reasonable in light of everything else, or does it appear inappropriate in these circumstances? Will it hinder your spiritual progress in any way? Will it offend another Christian or cause him or her to stumble or be made weak? As the Bible says, "The prudent considers well his steps" (Proverbs 14:15).

8. *Seek to please God, not people.* Is your decision being influenced by a desire to please other people, such as your family, a friend, or a coworker? Are you afraid of what others will think? Will you feel guilty if they disapprove of your decision? "The fear of man brings a snare, but whoever trusts in the LORD shall be safe" (Proverbs 29:25).

9. *Seek counsel from godly people.* God has given you a valuable resource in the counsel of mature, spiritually-minded

Christian friends. Ask for their advice and listen to what they say, considering what you can gain from their wisdom and experience. "Where there is no counsel the people fall, but in the multitude of counselors there is safety" (Proverbs 11:14).

10. *Consider your circumstances, but be careful not to depend too much upon them in discerning God's leading.* Although Gideon discovered God's will by "putting out the fleece" (Judges 6:36–40), God is under no obligation to honor such requests. Be cautious about this method of determining what God wants you to do. "For we walk by faith, not by sight" (2 Corinthians 5:7).

11. *Prepare and pray over a balance sheet.* After taking the preceding steps, write down both the positive and negative aspects of the decision you are facing—the pros and cons as well as the implications of each choice. Wrestle with them and pray over them for a few days, if possible, before making your decision. "A man's heart plans his way, but the LORD directs his steps" (Proverbs 16:9).

12. *Make a decision, wait for inner peace, and step out.* Do not be in a hurry. Most decisions can be approached cautiously and deliberately, but eventually, you must act. God will show you the way, either by opening or closing doors of opportunity, arranging circumstances in your favor, or providing new ideas and impressions to guide you. The Holy Spirit will give you a peaceful, lasting assurance if you are moving in God's will. "Trust in the Lord with all your heart, and lean not on your own understanding; in all your ways acknowledge Him, and He shall direct your paths" (Proverbs 3:5–6).

The Real Meaning
of Christmas

. . . .

"For there is born to you this day in the city of David
a Savior, who is Christ the Lord."
—Luke 2:11

["The Real Meaning of Christmas" was my first gospel tract, written
in 1976 and sent as a Christmas card to share the good news of Jesus
Christ with our extended family. Scripture quotations are taken from
the King James Version.]

Christmas is a season of joy and anticipation, a time for sending holiday
greetings and exchanging gifts with friends and loved ones. Christmas
means family gatherings, good food, special music, and seasonal events
of all kinds. But suppose that all of these were taken away. Would there
be any hint of Christmas remaining?

The simple truth of Christmas is that on this day, a Savior was
born—Christ the Lord. To deny this truth is to deny Jesus Christ.
While we may not do this willfully, when we fail to recognize and
honor Christ, we do, in fact, deny Him. How sad it is that for so many,
Christmas is over when the presents have been opened and the dinner
has been eaten. In many homes, Jesus Christ has no significant part in
the celebration of Christmas—His birthday! The Bible stories of Jesus'

birth are not read or told to the children, and His name is not even mentioned.

Our celebration of this great holiday must include, above all else, the recognition of the Savior, which is Christ the Lord. We need to give thanks to God and honor Jesus Christ throughout this special season! While we may enjoy the gifts and other material blessings of Christmas, our true focus must be upon the source of these blessings—our heavenly Father and His Son, Jesus Christ. As the Bible says, "Every good gift and every perfect gift is from above, and cometh down from the Father of lights, with whom is no variableness, neither shadow of turning" (James 1:17).

Jesus said, "Whoever confesses me before men, Him I will also confess before my Father who is in heaven. But whoever denies me before men, him I will also deny before my Father who is in heaven" (Matthew 10:32–33). Let us not be guilty of denying Christ by excluding Him from Christmas, but instead, let our attitude be that of the apostle Paul, who wrote, "For I am not ashamed of the gospel of Christ: for it is the power of God unto salvation to everyone that believeth; to the Jew first, and also to the Greek" (Romans 1:16).

"And she shall bring forth a Son, and thou shalt call his name JESUS: for He shall save His people from their sins." —Matthew 1:21

This is the message that the whole world needs to hear and understand, the real truth about Christmas! God came into the world as a babe, born of a virgin in a manger in Bethlehem. Thirty-three years later, He died on the cross, bearing the punishment for our sins. He arose from the grave on the third day, appeared to His disciples and ascended to heaven, where He now sits at the right hand of God. Our salvation cost God the life of His Son, yet it is free to us, if we will only turn from our sins in repentance and accept this great gift.

Have you trusted Jesus Christ as your Lord and Savior? If not, what better time is there than now to receive Him into your life and to share the message of salvation with others? The Bible says, "I have heard thee in a time accepted, and in the day of salvation have I helped thee: behold, now is the accepted time; behold, now is the day of salvation" (2 Corinthians 6:2).

What a Christmas this can be if you will accept God's greatest gift! As the Bible says, "For by grace are ye saved through faith; and that not of yourselves: it is the gift of God: not of works, lest any man should boast" (Ephesians 2:8–9), "For God so loved the world, that he gave His only begotten Son, that whosoever believeth in Him should not perish, but have everlasting life" (John 3:16), and "But as many as received Him, to them gave He power to become the sons of God, even to them that believe on His name" (John 1:12).

Dear friend, will you give Christ His rightful place this Christmas? Read the stories of Jesus' birth, found in Matthew and Luke, and share them with your family. Thank God for His great love and His great gift, and you will experience the real meaning of Christmas!

Signs of Life

* *

"Examine yourselves to see whether you
are in the faith; test yourselves.
Do you not realize that Christ Jesus is in you—
unless, of course, you fail the test?"
2 Corinthians 13:5

[Scripture quotations are taken from the *Holy Bible: New International Version.*]

If you are a Christian, you have experienced a profound and permanent change in your life. You have become a new creature in Christ Jesus. You have been "born again." But how can you be sure? First of all, even if you do not know exactly when you were saved, you should still be able to identify the period of time when your life began to change as a result of your decision to follow Christ. Secondly, just as there are "vital signs"—pulse, respiration, temperature, etc.—that reveal the existence of physical life, there are signs that indicate the presence of spiritual life. The purpose of this booklet is to introduce these "spiritual vital signs." If they are missing from your life, you should question the validity of your Christian experience.

A New Kind of Awareness

When we receive Christ into our lives, the Holy Spirit imparts an "inner light" that awakens us to spiritual realities: "God made His light shine in our hearts" (2 Corinthians 4:6). If you do not know Christ, you may think that you have this inner light when, in fact, you do not. You may mistake some lesser experience for "the real thing," such as the impact on your life of some emotion-packed worship service or a familiarity with Christianity gained from godly parents and lifelong church attendance. Yet after getting saved, people with these and other mistaken ideas about salvation freely admit that they did not have the light at all. At best, they had only "head knowledge" of salvation. There was no experience to back up their claim to have received the light.

This inner light may come gradually, like the dawning of the day, or instantly, as when a dark room is illuminated by the flip of a switch. Either way, the light appears, and we come alive spiritually. Charles Colson describes his experience as such:

> There came a sureness of mind… a wonderful new assurance about life, a fresh perception of myself and the world around me. I was coming alive to things I had never seen before… a whole new kind of awareness.[12]

Through His quiet, inward activity, the Holy Spirit imparts spiritual life and then assures us of our new relationship with God. As the Bible says, "The Spirit himself testifies with our spirit that we are God's children" (Romans 8:16). Have you experienced a new assurance about life—a whole new kind of awareness?

Restfulness in Your Mind

Most people have a natural, though often unrecognizable, desire for peace with God. There is something missing from our lives, leaving a void that only God can fill. On a television talk show, a well-known Hollywood celebrity said, "I am terrified of death!" The cause of such fear, anxiety, and restlessness is basically sin, and here we are all in the same boat. We have sinned and alienated ourselves from God. But the Lord Jesus Christ came to take care of this problem. He suffered and died for our sins to blot them out in God's sight, then he arose from the dead. Until Christ comes into our lives, we remain in a state of unforgiveness, condemnation, and guilt.

The Bible says, "Since we have been justified through faith, we have peace with God through our Lord Jesus Christ" (Romans 5:1). Being "justified through faith" means to be absolved from the penalty of sin and restored to a right relationship with God. In the heart of every Christian, there will be peace—a restfulness of mind concerning life, death, and eternity. After experiencing this peace from God, John Wesley said, "I felt my heart strangely warmed."[13] This peace that passes understanding has a way of warming the heart in a strange, but wonderful, way. Has your heart been strangely warmed? Do you have restfulness in your mind?

A Desire to Please God

The Bible says, "There is now no condemnation for those who are in Christ Jesus" (Romans 8:1). Yet our claim to be in Christ Jesus, and under no condemnation because we have been saved, is only valid if it is supported by a life that reflects our new relationship with God. After we accept Christ, we want to obey God. We may not think of it as a yearning for "holiness" or "godliness." We may simply desire to please God. As believers, we are faced with a whole new standard for living—a standard that is much higher than just what our natural instincts tell us about right and wrong. Chances are that our initial concept of sin is simply "what we do wrong" or "what we fail to do right." Later, we discover that sin also includes every thought and attitude that is displeasing to God, anything that is contrary to His will and character. Eventually, we come to realize that apart from the Holy Spirit's working in our lives, we are altogether incapable of obeying God or becoming like Christ. Every Christian struggles with sin, so where there is no struggle, no conviction of sin, no sense of guilt, and no desire to change, there also may be no spiritual life. Are you satisfied with your life or are you striving to be like Christ?

A Thirsty Soul

Just as our bodies can develop a thirst that only water can satisfy, the Holy Spirit produces a spiritual thirst in our lives that only God can satisfy. The psalmist expresses it well, saying, "O God, you are my God, earnestly I seek you; my soul thirsts for you, my body longs for you, in a dry and weary land where there is no water" (Psalm 63:1). His whole being yearns for communion with God. Without this fellowship, his life is as dry as a thirsty desert. Spiritual life requires spiritual nourishment, which comes from the Word of God. Yet many people who claim to know Christ will admit that they seldom read the Bible, even though they are involved in church and Christian activities.

Worship and fellowship with other believers is important, but it is no substitute for communion with God. Even ministry to people, an essential part of the Christian life, must not take precedence over prayer and time spent in the Word of God. To the contrary, a strong devotional life provides the power for effective ministry. A lasting desire to read and study the Bible is a sure sign of the Spirit's presence in our lives. If we bear God's name, we should find joy and delight in his Word: "When your words came, I ate them; they were my joy and my heart's delight, for I bear your name, O LORD God Almighty" (Jeremiah 15:16). Can you say, like Job, "I have treasured the words of his mouth more than my necessary food?" (Job 23:12). Does your devotional life—the time you spend in the Bible and prayer—validate your claim to be a Christian?

An Interest in Spiritual Things

The Bible says, "For we are to God the aroma of Christ among those who are being saved… the fragrance of life" (2 Corinthians 2:15–16). As followers of Jesus Christ, we will be drawn to other believers by the fragrance of Christ's life. We will have a natural interest in spiritual things as well as a desire for fellowship with other Christians. Where is your "spiritual comfort zone"? Does it extend beyond the church building or outside of your home? Are you comfortable talking about

God and spiritual things in the workplace, at the grocery store, or in the neighborhood? Some who claim to be Christians appear to have no spiritual comfort zone. It is difficult, if not impossible, to carry on a conversation with them about God or Jesus Christ. They show little evidence that they know Christ or that God plays a significant role in their lives.

What is the reason for this lack of interest in spiritual matters? It may be that they do not possess the Holy Spirit, for it is only by the Spirit that we can understand and accept spiritual truth: "The man without the Spirit does not accept the things that come from the Spirit of God, for they are foolishness to him, and he cannot understand them because they are spiritually discerned" (1 Corinthians 2:14). As for the unbeliever, the Bible says, "In all his thoughts there is no room for God" (Psalm 10:4). Is God in your mind and thoughts? Is His name on your lips? Beware if you have no interest in spiritual things!

Compassion for People

The day I accepted Christ, I spoke with a friend about becoming a Christian. Though I was not yet prepared for such an encounter, I did not question whether it was the right thing to do. I had found life, and with it came a desire to talk to others about Christ. The Bible says, "Let the redeemed of the LORD say so" (Psalm 107:2). Since Christ came into the world to save sinners, it is through this expression of the Holy Spirit—compassion toward people—that we can participate in God's plan of salvation for the human race. His plan includes using Christians to bear the good news of Jesus Christ. Billy Graham says this:

> We Christians have the Word of God. We are holding a light. We are blowing a trumpet. We are kindling a fire, striking with a hammer, using a sword. We have bread for a hungry world. We have water for a famishing people. We must keep standing and crying out: 'Everyone that thirsts, come to the waters.'[14]

The Bible tells a story of some lepers who found a large supply of food and drink in a time of great famine. The men who had leprosy "said to each other: 'We're not doing right. This is a day of good news and we are keeping it to ourselves. If we wait until daylight, punishment will overtake us. Let's go at once and report this to the royal palace'" (2 Kings 7:8–9). The message of Christ is for everyone! Like the lepers, if you are a Christian, you cannot keep this good news to yourself. This sign of life is that you now possess a God-given compassion toward those who are perishing, as well as toward the poor and needy. Do your attitude and actions demonstrate a genuine concern for the eternal well-being of others? If not, why not? Are you a real Christian?

If you are a Christian, you should recognize in yourself these signs of spiritual life. An inner light given to you by the Holy Spirit testifies that you have been born again; the peace that accompanies this light brings assurance that your sins have been forgiven. The Holy Spirit has put within you a desire to be like Christ, along with a hunger for the Bible, God's Word. An interest in spiritual things, a desire to fellowship with other believers, and compassion toward people are further distinguishing marks of a genuine Christian.

The Bible says, "And this is the testimony: God has given us eternal life, and this life is in His Son. He who has the Son has life; he who does not have the Son of God does not have life. I write these things to you who believe in the name of the Son of God so that you may know that you have eternal life" (1 John 5:11–13).

If you are not certain that you have Jesus Christ in your life, sincerely pray this prayer right now, and He will come in: "Lord Jesus, I am a sinner, and I cannot save myself. I believe that You died on the cross for my sins and were raised from the dead. Please forgive me, come into my life as Savior and Lord, and give me the gift of eternal life."

Appendix: List of Tracts and Booklets

* *

The following publications, as well as a description of each, can be obtained from the author at fcoint@windstream.net or by sending a request to 1401 Longview Drive, Campbellsville, KY 42718.

Tracts

Can You Afford to Wait?
Making Right Choices
Our Eyes: A Christian Perspective
Share Christ through Tract Evangelism
The Witness of the Heavens

Booklets

A Handbook of New Testament Terms, People, and Places
Home at Last
How to Have an Effective Quiet Time
Life in the Marketplace
Mysteries of the Kingdom: A Look at the Parables of Jesus
Signs of Life
The Doctrine of Rewards
The Kings of Israel and Judah
The Meaning of Greatness
The Problem of Tares
Where Is Your Brother?

Endnotes

1   Mullins, E.Y., *Why Is Christianity True?* (Chicago, IL: Christian Culture Press, 1905), 294–295.

2   Hill, Dwight, "Facts of the Matter" (http://www.factsofthematter.org.) September 29, 2004.

3   Manning, Brennan, *Ruthless Trust* (New York, NY: Harper Collins, 2000), 13.

4   MacDonald, William, *True Discipleship* (Kansas City, KS: Walterick Publishers, 1975), 5.

5   Stott, John, *Basic Christianity* (Downers Grove, IL: InterVarsity Press, 1958), 112.

6   Trotman, Dawson, *Born to Reproduce* (Colorado Springs, CO: NavPress, 1974), 24.

7   Paraphrased from Adsit, Christopher, *Personal Disciplemaking* (Orlando, FL: Campus Crusade for Christ, 1996), 41.

8   Ibid., 347.

9   Skinner, Betty Lee, *Daws* (Grand Rapids, MI: Zondervan, 1974), 39–40.

10 "The devotional" refers to Walter Henrichsen's book, *Thoughts from the Diary of a Desperate Man,* published in 1999 by Leadership Foundation.

11 We lived in Brookhaven, Mississippi during the period 1982–1985.

12 Colson, Charles W., *Born Again* (Old Tappan, N.J.: Fleming H. Revell Co., 1976), 130.

13 Lean, Garth, *Strangely Warmed: The Amazing Life of John Wesley* (Tyndale House Publishers, 1982), 46.

14 Graham, Billy, *Peace with God* (Old Tappan, N.J.: Fleming H. Revell Co., 1953), 155–156.